SAGE was founded in 1965 by Sara Miller McCune to support the dissemination of usable knowledge by publishing innovative and high-quality research and teaching content. Today, we publish more than 750 journals, including those of more than 300 learned societies, more than 800 new books per year, and a growing range of library products including archives, data, case studies, reports, conference highlights, and video. SAGE remains majority-owned by our founder, and after Sara's lifetime will become owned by a charitable trust that secures our continued independence.

Los Angeles | London | Washington DC | New Delhi | Singapore | Boston

Brave New Bollywood

Brave New Bollywood

In Conversation with Contemporary Hindi Filmmakers

Nirmal Kumar
Preeti Chaturvedi

www.sagepublications.com
Los Angeles • London • New Delhi • Singapore • Washington DC • Boston

Copyright © Nirmal Kumar and Preeti Chaturvedi, 2015

All rights reserved. No part of this book may be reproduced or utilized in any form or by any means, electronic or mechanical, including photocopying, recording or by any information storage or retrieval system, without permission in writing from the publisher.

First published in 2015 by

SAGE Publications India Pvt Ltd
B1/I-1 Mohan Cooperative Industrial Area
Mathura Road, New Delhi 110 044, India
www.sagepub.in

SAGE Publications Inc
2455 Teller Road
Thousand Oaks, California 91320, USA

SAGE Publications Ltd
1 Oliver's Yard, 55 City Road
London EC1Y 1SP, United Kingdom

SAGE Publications Asia-Pacific Pte Ltd
3 Church Street
#10-04 Samsung Hub
Singapore 049483

Published by Vivek Mehra for SAGE Publications India Pvt Ltd, typeset in 11/13 Book Antiqua by RECTO Graphics, Delhi and printed at Saurabh Printers Pvt Ltd, New Delhi.

Library of Congress Cataloging-in-Publication Data Available

ISBN: 978-93-515-0031-5 (HB)

The SAGE Team: Shambhu Sahu, Isha Sachdeva, Nand Kumar Jha and Dally Verghese

For Ritu
~Nirmal Kumar

For Nana–Nani,
who idolized Dilip Kumar and Madhubala –
the way very few can.

For Ashutosh,
who taught me the meaning of good cinema.

For Ma, Papa and Sunny,
for being crazy about cinema and otherwise!

And above all, for my darling daughter
who is more beautiful than any work of art.
~Preeti Chaturvedi

Thank you for choosing a SAGE product! If you have any comment, observation or feedback, I would like to personally hear from you. Please write to me at contactceo@sagepub.in

—Vivek Mehra, Managing Director and CEO,
SAGE Publications India Pvt Ltd, New Delhi

Bulk Sales

SAGE India offers special discounts for purchase of books in bulk. We also make available special imprints and excerpts from our books on demand.

For orders and enquiries, write to us at

Marketing Department
SAGE Publications India Pvt Ltd
B1/I-1, Mohan Cooperative Industrial Area
Mathura Road, Post Bag 7
New Delhi 110044, India
E-mail us at marketing@sagepub.in

Get to know more about SAGE, be invited to SAGE events, get on our mailing list. Write today to marketing@sagepub.in

This book is also available as an e-book.

Contents

Brave New Bollywood: An Introduction   ix

Dibakar Banerjee   1
Of Milieu, Technique and the Dialectic of Anti-dumb Cinema

Kiran Rao   43
The Personal as the Voyeur – The Aesthetics of Meaning

Reema Kagti   87
Collaboration and Commerce – Treading the Thin Line

Zoya Akhtar   115
Urban and Unapologetic – The Cinema of Zoya Akhtar

Shonali Bose   139
Loss and Survival – The Cinema of Meaning

Anusha Rizvi   181
Content as King – How Stories Create Filmmakers

Onir   205
The Politics at the Margins – Being an Alternative Filmmaker in Bollywood

Tigmanshu Dhulia   **241**
*The Alternative as Mainstream – Blurring the
Boundaries in Cinematic Tradition*

About the Authors   271

Brave New Bollywood: An Introduction

These are interesting times in the history of Indian cinema, particularly because the established aesthetic conventions and modes of production of the Hindi film industry are being challenged as are the boundaries between what is alternative and mainstream. A new idiom is emerging — which, to borrow the phrase from Dibakar Banerjee, is that of anti-dumb cinema. The attempt of this book is to contextualize the upsurge in a certain form of cinema in Bollywood, which is both alternative yet mainstream, through an understanding of the sociological underpinnings of the men and women who make these movies.

The defining characteristic of these movies is their uncompromising story, which creates a world of fallible yet believable characters. The audience, however, remains the Indian middle class — a viable synergy since the financial models of these movies make sense in a multiplex ecosphere, which again are increasingly becoming the new middle-class hang outs. It is difficult to say whether the genre of meaningful cinema is coming into its own, or the very realm of what we hitherto called 'mainstream' is expanding to become more inclusive.

Historical Overview

The cinema of new sensibility builds upon the sensibility of the 'experimental cinema' with its many historical precedents in the form of the New Cinema Movement, which started in the late sixties. Although there was no possibility of a significant popular success of experimental films at that time, their continued production under the supportive aegis of the government had long-term consequences on the Hindi mainstream industry.

Ravi Vasudevan observes that from the sixties onwards, parallel cinema emerged as the object of middle-class spectatorship, especially in the wake of the 'massification' of the commercial form into an encompassing and alienating package of spectacle, action and titillation (Vasudevan, 2000).

Right from the seventies, there has been the possibility of a substantial segment of the middle-class audience drifting towards an alternative cultural space (Prasad, 2001). Much of the parallel cinema of the seventies and eighties was made in Hindi, although it is linked to other art cinemas in many Indian languages, particularly Bengali and Malayalam. This cinema was instrumental in generating a spate of writing by filmmakers about the movement of which they themselves were a part (Dwyer & Pinto, 2011).

It has also been argued by scholars that there is a Middle Cinema, one that literally stands between popular and the elite art cinema. It is aimed at a large section of the middle-class audience, which is a product of the urban boom. Although this Middle Cinema tackles important issues, it is the treatment that differentiates this genre from both popular and world cinema (Gokulsing & Dissayanaker, 1998).

This cinema is having a second lease of life with the anti-dumb cinema of our times—this time, though, in a more commercially viable manner. This cinema is characterized by a new social language. Gender roles are questioned. Social structures are laid bare in all their hypocrisies. Moreover, movies such as *LSD: Love, Sex Aur Dhokha* and *Luck By Chance* have pushed the envelope further by turning the gaze inwards, critiquing the whole concept of media, movies and voyeurism per se.

What Is Mainstream?

The important question remains where to place this new genre of cinema—on the periphery of mainstream, characterized as 'alternative' or accommodate it within the very mainstream after the category has been redefined. Bollywood cinema has been marked by a simplistic and almost dogmatic style of narrative where good wins over evil, the feudal value system is reinforced and gender stereotypes are consolidated—the perfect antithesis of everything that this contemporary cinema stands for.

Many critics such as Gokulsing and Dissanayake have traditionally drawn an analogy between Indian popular films and morality plays, 'where good triumphs over evil and the social order disrupted by the actions of immoral and villainous people is restored by the power of goodness. Entertainment and moral edification are combined in a way that has direct appeal to the vast masses of moviegoers' (Gokulsing & Dissayanaker, 1998).

Researchers and social scientists have observed that while art cinema is finding a larger audience base, popular cinema is gaining acceptance in the film festival circles (Nandy & Lal, 2005).

The question arises, does one consider alternative cinema as part of the larger mainstream or as a critical response to dominant modes of representation in mainstream cinema (Ghosh, 2011)?

Overview of the Project

This book was primarily conceived as an oral history project. It was meant for the students of South Asia and cinema studies who would research South Asian society and culture. It is intended as a primer on some of the filmmakers included in this volume. While there is a lot of literature available on contemporary cinema through reviews and more serious academic critiques, there is very little available on directors. Hence, a first-person account by younger filmmakers about what went on in their life and mind is important for a deeper understanding of cinema.

The aim of this project was to promote an academic enquiry into the educational and family background of these avant-garde filmmakers, their religious beliefs, social moorings, cinematic influences, attitude towards filmmaking and experiences of making the film/s. For a researcher, it may be necessary to get into the bio-narrative to decipher the person and his/her filmmaking. What we see is actually just the final outcome of a long creative process which is more often than not quite unrelated with the creativity that makes filmmaking a passion. On the other hand, the creativity of the process of filmmaking involves a duality of discursive process that involves the best of technology and creativity.

What one visualizes and what the current and affordable level of technology translates into frames are two parallel progressions that need to meet in the process of filmmaking. This is not only natural but also inevitable and this differentiates cinema from other kinds of performing arts where actors perform before an inanimate camera. When it comes to cinema, all cinema needs to be retouched in a complex and technically advanced post-production process. And hence all creativity must be in discursive conjunction with technology. It is not only important to act but equally important to act in sync with technology and act in bursts. In onstage or any other performance, the whole set up has to move with the narration, but in films, it is only a small frame that gets filmed at a time. This gives ample time to improvize and yet has a tremendous lack of feel of the script. In India, where films are rarely shot according to bound scripts, constant improvization goes on while on the set, either due to directors or stars who are prone to dictate changes in everything from dialogues to scene to set to make up. More often than not, even in this disjointed and impulsive kind of filmmaking, it is only the director who knows what is happening.

Hence, it becomes imperative for a student of cinema studies to know the director well. The directors interviewed in this volume have a commonality in cinematic ideology. At the risk of oversimplification, what we imply is that these filmmakers are united by their vision of producing true-to-life realistic cinema where story is the king. The budget might be small or big; some of their movies might even be marked by the presence of megastars; nonetheless, it is the cinematic portrayal which distinguishes these moviemakers from others.

Another basis for selection is that in their own ways, their cinema has been instrumental in changing the very dynamics of the film industry. Insofar as that, these movies and moviemakers have become cult figures in themselves forging a new canon of creative disruption.

The Role of the Director

The new breed of directors with their tight scripts, apt casting and realistic treatment of storyline have come to stay and are making fundamental changes to the very nature of

Hindi cinema and its supporting industry structures. These moviemakers, backed by the strength of their storytelling and sculpted dialogue, have reinvigorated the art of cinema with a newfound health.

Films are mostly, at least in India, known by the stars who act in them. Mostly people are unaware of the technical team responsible for making of the film. Not many would actually remember the names of the directors of films such as *Mahal*, *Howrah Bridge*, *Guide* or even *Mughal-e-Azam*. In recent times, directors have started taking the centre stage during film promotions. Media savvy filmmakers such as Dibakar Banerjee, Karan Johar or Imtiaz Ali have been giving scores of interviews to all who care to watch and have become a recognizable commodity. Today, much like yesteryear's Salim–Javed, among scriptwriters, there are directors who are recognized by their names and films are sold in their names. Much like their French counterparts, they are recognized as auteurs, whose stamp sells films of a particular type. Indian filmmakers have also taken pro-active steps to style themselves auteurs with a particular brand of filmmaking. Avant-garde filmmakers such as Shyam Benegal and Govind Nihalani, and now Tigmanshu Dhulia and Dibakar Banerjee, are known to make a particular kind of cinema that audiences easily identify with. Most notable in this category is Anurag Kashyap who is the front runner of the new wave cinema in India today.

These makers, new and still active, share a world of experiences, sometimes same, mostly unique. The book addresses many questions that a serious researcher or a keen reader is likely to have — what goes into the making of a filmmaker? Why does one choose films as the medium of expression amongst so many?

Regionalism and Urbanism

The current idiom of filmmaking is part of the vernacular forces thrown up by the new democratic order which has a very interesting relationship with urban India. It appeals to the upwardly mobile, English-speaking middle class while depicting rural or semi-rural India and its inhabitants as its subjects. The cinema of the carnivalesque with its larger than life characters, melodramatic orientation and highly romanticized canvas is giving way to the cinema of more relatable storylines, with characters that one can connect with and settings that are more believable. The semi-urban and rural consciousness is also pervading the art form. Even urban reality being depicted is increasingly showcasing more fallible and life-like characters. Interestingly, the former format of movies is still surviving—as showcased by the 100 Crore Club.

New Infrastructure

The availability of exhibition spaces is allowing experimental cinema to become viable. The lack of screen density and the dominion of single screen theatres meant that the true potential of cinema was not being explored so far. With the introduction of multiplexes, this ecosystem has seen a shift.

Despite 11,500 active screens, India is still under-screened. One of the largest entertainment markets, China, produces far lesser films than India but has 65,000 screens, while the US has 36,000 screens. India's screen density stands at a very low figure of 12 screens per million. There is a need for at least 20,000 screens as against the current 11,500. This gives multiplex operators enough room to grow as traditional single-screen theatres lack the financial muscle.[1]

Nonetheless, the emergence of multiplexes has given a thrust to content-driven movies, which are produced on tight budgets and popularized largely through word-of-mouth marketing. In some cases, though, production houses work on tight operating margins and sleek budgets eventually pumping in money into film promotion to give it the feel of a big-budget movie.

These movies have become viable owing to theatres with low seating capacities that now allow for cost-effective screening. Growing urbanization has fuelled the taste of an increasingly refined audience which can connect with this kind of cinema.

The trend of 'multiplex cinema' is different from the earlier new wave cinema in a few aspects:

1. From the nineties there has been a visible spurt in the number of multi-screen complexes called multiplexes where more than one screen is installed with lesser seating capacity but new seats and acoustics, and high entry prices.
2. The smaller number of seats ensured that relatively small and independent films could afford to be released in a theatre.

This trend started with Dibakar Bannerjee's *Khosla ka Ghosla* and *LSD: Love, Sex Aur Dhokha* and Sagar Bellary's *Bheja Fry*, whereby small films with no big stars, item songs or mega-budget advertising became hugely successful.

1. http://www.stockmarketsreview.com/extras/multiplex_companies_in_india_are_offering_a_bouquet_of_innovative_services_to_lure_people_20111209_217756/

The expression 'small film' is used here both because of its small budget and non-existent star cast. Small cinema does not necessarily mean small number of viewers but rather the scale of economies involved. The new cinema popularly called multiplex cinema fits the bill of 'small film' rather well. Story, deft camerawork and refreshing direction are the keywords. These films hardly have the budget for mega publishing drives; they mostly run on reviews and new media. The success of recent films such as *Vicky Donor* has surprised all. The new multiplexes have shown that small cinemas can be a success with the right mix of story, direction and target audience. However, this cinema might not draw a large audience (Athique & Hill, 2010).

However, of late it has been noticed that these small-budget movies are facing a tough time even in the exhibition space as mega movies such as *Ghajini*, *Dabangg* and *Singham* have monopolized even these spaces.

References

Athique A. and Hill D. *The Multiplex in India: A Cultural Economy of Urban Leisure*. London & New York: Routledge, 2010.

Dwyer R. and Pinto J. *Beyond the Boundaries of Bollywood*. New Delhi: Oxford University Press, 2011, p. Xvii.

Ghosh M. Alternative Cinema: Response of Indian Film Studies. *Journal of the Moving Image*, 2011 (http://www.jmionline.org/articles/2011/alternative_cinema_response_of_indian_film_studies.pdf).

Gokulsing M. and Dissayanaker W. *Indian Popular Cinema: A Narrative of Cultural Change*. New Delhi: Orient Longman, 1998.

Nandy A. and Lal V. *Fingerprinting Popular Culture*. New Delhi: Viking Penguin, 2005, pp. Xii–Xiii.

Prasad, M. M. *Ideology of the Hindi Film: A Historical Construction*. Oxford: Oxford University Press, 2001.

Vasudevan R. *Making Meaning in Indian Cinema*. New Delhi: Oxford University Press, 2000.

Dibakar Banerjee

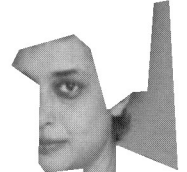
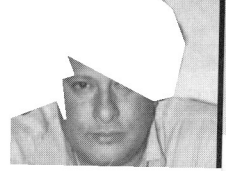

Source: Authors.

A force to reckon with, self-fashioned director and screenwriter, Dibakar Banerjee is one of the leading filmmakers of young Bollywood. Brought up on a culturally wholesome diet of literature, Hindustani music and art, Dibakar belongs to a typical Bengali household. He lived with his parents and elder sister on New Rohtak Road, and though he led a sheltered life, this slightly wary nine-year-old Bengali boy was no stranger to the ways of the upwardly mobile Punjabi community. To be an intellectual was not enough, so Dibakar ran around with a lot of rough kids and soaked in the West Delhi culture of Karol Bagh.

Toeing the line in school, Dibakar began to carve a separate identity for himself at the young age of 16. He cleared competitive entrance tests and secured admission to the prestigious National Institute of Design (NID), Ahmedabad. The place opened up an exciting, new world of music and cinema for him, but a year-and-a-half into the Visual Communication and Graphic Design programme, Dibakar felt he had learned enough and subsequently he dropped out. Next, he excelled as a copywriter for a string for ad-film production houses, but ever restless, in 1997, he started his own production company, Watermark, along with two other friends. His Midas touch prevailed yet again, but never one to rest on his laurels, Banerjee decided to pursue a passion he had nursed all along—creating the kind of Hindi cinema that mattered to him.

A call from scriptwriter Jaideep Sahni crystallized this dream and led to Dibakar Banerjee's directorial debut, *Khosla ka Ghosla* (2006). Set in Delhi, the film traces the story of an earnest, middle-class man's (Anupam Kher) quest to reclaim his plot of land, usurped by a crafty, real estate shark (Boman Irani). Intuitive yet clear-sighted, it converses as much with the changing structures of family and the ensuing generation gap as it does with the changing notions of affluence. Feted by critics, the film also resonated with urban audiences and won the National Film Award for the Best Feature Film in Hindi (2006). With his first film itself, Banerjee proved that he could, effortlessly, straddle the two disparate worlds of 'popular' Hindi cinema and independent filmmaking.

While *Khosla ka Ghosla* was a sympathetic portrayal of the middle class often cheated out of its hard-earned wealth, his next venture *Oye Lucky! Lucky Oye!* (2008) starring Abhay Deol and Paresh Rawal exposed the hypocrisy of an aspirational class, always craving for something better, even at the cost of its most intimate relationships. This time the viewer was led to identify with a crooked thief who desired the finer things just like any other ambitious middle-class person, thereby opening up a fresh perspective on social mobility. For the second time Banerjee bagged the National Film Award, this one for the Best Popular Film.

Banerjee's next undertaking, *LSD: Love, Sex Aur Dhokha* (2010), is a caustic simulation of regressive objectification and its consumption in a deeply voyeuristic society that is redefining its moral limits. The film narrates three linked stories through the medium of handheld cameras and CCTV footage. Though a critical and commercial success, Banerjee faced the misplaced ire of the censor board, for *LSD: Love, Sex Aur Dhokha* purported smuttiness, and the disappointment of many viewers due to the absence of raunch and sensationalism.

Dibakar's foray into Bollywood was not a struggle by any means, as he honestly admits himself. Financially, he was secure owing to the capital he had accumulated during his years at advertising agencies. Also, his wife Richa's steady and well-paid corporate job acted as a reliable buffer. But none of this made Dibakar even remotely complacent.

He is one director who is always judicious with the producer's money. His marketing mantra is simple, that is, make small-budget films that appear big and hold the imagination of the audience.

The political thriller, *Shanghai* (2012), Banerjee's fourth venture, lives up to his magic mantra where the gilded backdrop of the film is far more opulent than the actual cost of production. Inspired by Vassilis Vassilikos's novel 'Z', the sinister *Shanghai* is a world hurtling towards illusory modern 'progress' in the garb of development. It is the tale of a small town that is relentless in its pursuit of becoming a developed city, prosperous and swanky, at the cost of the impoverished classes. Yet again, Banerjee provides an engaging commentary on society, though this time it is dark and gloomy.

Banerjee's most recent experiment is the short film *Star*, one of the four short films that form *Bombay Talkies*, an anthology that is a tribute to the centenary year of Hindi cinema. An adaptation of Satyajit Ray's short story, *Patol Babu, Film Star*, it is a moving account of a failed actor (Nawazuddin Siddiqui) who gets one final chance to fulfil his dream and prove himself to his daughter. The common thread that weaves through his body of work is that here too, Dibakar Banerjee debunks the categories of 'mainstream' and 'art' cinema and confirms that some artists cannot be pigeonholed.

Of Milieu, Technique and the Dialectic of Anti-dumb Cinema

Preeti: *Do you think the role of cinema is also to offer deep psychological insights into the human condition?*

Dibakar: Somehow, in India, everything becomes either wide-eyed videography or extremely pedantic. There is a 'Masters Series' that is very famous amongst us—film professionals. This famous alternative filmmaker, every once in a while, goes and interviews 12 directors. It is open, anything under the sun; for example, Sidney Pollock just talks about how he directs his scene and what he comes prepared with when he is about to shoot a scene. It is fascinating to read. The essence of 30 years of his filmmaking, of his tradecraft, is out there to see and read, because ultimately, I feel, only tradecraft talked of passionately can open up deep psychological insights. If you start with psychological insights you will see connections that are force fitted but if you apply it from tradecraft, ultimately if you manage to reach that depth, it is a very good depth. Tradecraft-oriented stuff is very limited here in India. I am very enthusiastic about anything that is based on tradecraft, on approach, on work, on practice and preparation, and that which is based on simple objective things about the making of films. That which leads us to the bigger subjective issues rather than having to start with big, subjective and thematic concerns and then trying to fit things around that.

Nirmal: *You lived in New Rohtak Road and Karol Bagh, away from CR Park.*

Dibakar: Absolutely. The CR Park Bong (Bengali) immigration wave started, if you remember, in the late sixties, but it was only in the early seventies that the colony took root. It was called East Pakistan Displaced People's Colony. The CR Park Bengali immigration is a totally different phenomenon from the original Bengali migration to Delhi, which started in 1911 when the decision to shift the capital was taken. Between 1911 and 1931, the Old Secretariat used to be the head of the Delhi administration. So all the clerks and the *karkoon*s (record keepers) of the Hindustan *sarkar* (government) — the Governor's entire office — were shifted from Calcutta to Delhi. Obviously there were a lot of Bengalis.

The first colony that was constructed was the one around the Old Secretariat. The other colonies were Kashmere Gate, Darya Ganj and Minto Road. If you look at the history of *Durga puja* (goddess worship), and this is a fantastic subaltern history project, the founding of each of these *puja*s is itself a history of immigration of Bengalis into the city. The Kashmere Gate and Minto Road *Durga pujas* have been on since the 1920s. So you know that Bengalis came there first. Then from the thirties onwards came the New Delhi *puja* when the Parliament came up. Between the thirties and forties it was Mandir Marg and Gole Market, which were the next Bengali centres. Then you see Kali Bari, it was in the thirties or forties that it came up.

The Gole Market area had a solid Bengali population. It was the same with South Indians. All of this has got to do with government clerks and government jobs shifting to the Old Secretariat and then to the New Secretariat.

Nirmal: Did you miss out on your Bengali neighbourhood and Bengali influence?

Dibakar: No. My grandfather came to Delhi in 1950, and so we were the intermediate immigrant. He was in the Indian Army where he was a non-commissioned officer, a *Subedar* (Major), in the Ordinance department. He also fought the Japanese. He was there at the front in the Battle of Nagaland. He had seen trench warfare. One of my favourite stories as a kid told by my grandfather was the one in which he was in an L-shaped trench and there were two *hawaldar*s on the other side. One of them sneezed and a grenade was thrown in. I was four or five and he used to tell me these gory stories. He would use the Bengali term *chin bhin* to describe the devastation wrought on their bodies, and I was just a small kid.

Another story was that he was standing in Imphal where the last stand was taken by the British army (the Japanese onslaught was halted here) against the Japanese and Subhas Bose's INA—so they were fighting their own countrymen. He remember being stationed in Imphal. I wish I had recorded those stories because it is true history. He remembers being on the Company Captain's bike and rushing from one station to another to deliver a letter or a signal, and in between seeing the Jap troop movement, and turning and going through another route. Another story I still remember is that he saw a man who had been bayoneted coming down a mountain. All these stories were very interesting for a five-year-old boy.

Then in 1950, my grandfather moved to Delhi with my grandmother and my father, who was their only son. They first came to a resettlement camp for some reason, I don't know why, and started living in Shakurbasti, where they stayed for about a year-and-a-half. Then a great flood surged through Shakurbasti. So my father got hold of *Dalda ghee* tins, tied them up together, placed a plank on them and made a raft. Apparently, everyone would do that. We still have two or three small photographs of that at home. Then from Shakurbasti they moved to Rohtak Road. From the fifties till the eighties we kept moving to various houses around that area.

Nirmal: What was your childhood like?

Dibakar: My childhood was overprotected. My sister was eight years older than me. So I was literally the baby of the family. My sister used to mother me, my parents of course, and my grandfather whose life was centred around his grandchildren. Since my sister was now eight and was going to school, I was the one who was the darling of the house. I was extremely protected as a result of which I think I became a little namby-pamby. I had asthma so I was a little sickly, and also retiring and shy, basically *darpok* (easily scared). A firework would go off somewhere and I would run and hide in a room. So I was timid, sickly and given to imagination. I could sketch very well. My grandfather would get me practice sketchbooks since I was two or three. I think for a long time he had preserved my sketches. There were lions, tigers and cars.

My family was always into music and literature, so there were always books and music. My mother and sister are into classical music. My niece's mother teaches classical music at the Indira Gandhi National Open University (IGNOU).

Preeti: *So how did your relationship with your family evolve by the time you got into advertising and then when you were at NID? How did you see the dynamic change?*

The notion of the utopian Indian family, in a movie like Khosla ka Ghosla, *with the conformist son and the protective elder brother, despite the kind of avant-garde cinema that you make, remains intact. Ultimately, the family fabric is restored when the character played by Parvin Dabas decides to stick with the name given to him by his family, which is ridiculous, and he foregoes the opportunity of going abroad and pursuing his dreams. Somehow that is the happy family picture. So here is a director who makes* LSD: Love, Sex Aur Dhokha *but is still a conformist in many ways.*

Similarly, in Oye Lucky! Lucky Oye! *he is the thief with a heart of gold, but in a way he is also the protective, giving and selfless elder brother. Is this entire dynamic playing out at your subconscious level?*

Dibakar: You have hit the nail on the head with *Khosla ka Ghosla*. If you read my interview with Mihir Pandya in his book *Shahar Aur Cinema: Via Dilli*, which is about films centred in Delhi, you will understand. He got an extensive interview with me, by chance, because he used to write to me in Hindi and I used to write back to him in Hindi (I am good with the language).

Khosla ka Ghosla is my first film. It is as much my film as it is Jaideep Sahni, the scriptwriter's film. It would be an interesting exercise, if you can spare the time, and if it matches your format, to have a chat with Jaideep and see the making of the film through his eyes. He was there as a senior statesman—he was already writing scripts for Bollywood. At that time he had just written the script of *Company* and was awarded for that. He had introduced me to the producer and he was the man who pushed the film

Source: Authors.

forward. It was his vision to get a film done from Delhi with me as a director. He asked me if I would do it, to which I replied—only if you write it.

In 2002 or 2003 as I was writing the film along with Jaideep and in 2004 or 2003 as I was making the film I think the main thing that sprung out from me into the film was the guilt that you face at the age when you sever your connections with your family, and chart out your own new family. So that was the original guilt that I was trying to expiate through this first film. Of course, you take the outward package of social turmoil of a Nehruvian, Gandhian-era man fighting a new, modern, liberated India kind of a villain called Khurana where greed is not only open but it is actually good as Gordon Gekko says in *Wall Street*. He is unashamedly greedy and sticks to greed as a genuine tenet of life, whereas Khosla is saying something else—it is that pointless and dull sacrifice that you have to make time and again on a daily basis, what our fathers' generation did.

Preeti: *Do you think we as a society, are obsessed with 'sacrifice' where the fabric of the family is concerned? In Onir's movie,* I Am, *the Nandita Das story portrays a woman who wants to have a child but her husband doesn't. In an argument with him, she chides him for addressing the baby as 'it' lest the child abandons the father in his old age. This is a woman who is actually looking at artificial insemination and single motherhood as an option, and is still going back to regressive notions of parenting.*

Dibakar: That is probably a poignant and actually a very apt description of the many paradoxes that we carry in a character. A living, breathing character as a human 'I' where some of the truths that we want to be truths are our own discovery while some of the truths are unconsciously part of our heritage or a legacy or a dead weight that we have been given, which we are yet to question. Five years from now that woman will be saying that I am getting a child because I want the joy of bringing up a child for the next 15–20 years as a selfish way to live. The core need of parenthood is to have an innocent, baggage-less person to nurture in front of you because people are genetically hard-wired for that. But at that point when you are about to adopt or get artificially inseminated, you are thinking of a child and you are also trying to conform to the normal modes of parenthood, which justify your alternate behaviour. Therefore, you say that when the child gets older it will take care of its parents' happiness. I remember that scene and I think it is a good scene because it talks about the central paradox of the human condition.

Coming back to *Khosla ka Ghosla*—Jaideep and I both felt guilty about severing the link to the traditional, academic/job-oriented locus of an Indian middle-class family's male heir. We have broken that tradition 100%. I have broken that tradition three or four times. My family was deeply into Indian classical music and I know how to play the tabla. My mother has learned music from Naina devi and Chinmaya Roy, and now she is 75 but is still carrying on with her performances. Her misfortune to some extent was that she was also a Bengali housewife and had to hold the house together, so she could not go all out for a musical career. That is the lot of middle-class women—their sacrifice. She was a gold medallist in the All India Radio Sangeet Sammelan—with that you do not audition ever again to sing for the radio. They are natural inductees into the All India Radio at a 'B-High' grade. I know all this because to us this is our great heritage. *Maa* has done all this on her own merit. My mother, my sister and, now, my niece sing. So it is a solid family tradition. Somehow from class 6 or 7, I remember waking up deep, dead at night listening to BBC World Service and listening to Western classical, and I have no idea why. I still cannot figure it out because behind all these deviations lies some impetus. Someday I will discover why I did so. From there I veered away from my family tradition in Indian classical music. I went totally into Western classical first, then to Pop, and then Rock, Blues and Jazz. So I was totally steeped in the Western music tradition (of course, I had not left the Indian classical tradition). That was the first break.

The second break came when I moved away from academic excellence around class 10. I was reasonably okay till class 10 but after that I became spoilt. From always securing a position amongst the first four in class, I started coming 37th in a class of 40, or something like that. Of course, my class was a typical meritocratic class because those who choose the sciences are normally the class toppers. So from roll no. 1 to roll no. 40 there was no one with a percentage below 85%. You know what happened in schools especially in the late eighties. And in PCM (Physics, Chemistry, Maths) nobody scored less than 90%. So I was last in that. So that was the next break and my family realized that Dibakar was turning bad.

The third break was not sitting for any of the competitive exams, including the IITs. There was gentle pressure from my parents. But then they did not have an option. They did not know what I had in mind and neither did I. My father was a typical old-style ordinary graduate who had finished his education under extremely difficult conditions. He decided suddenly to uproot himself from Ranchi to come to Delhi, having to start his life all over again, time after time. He does not talk about it at all. Probably he is at peace with it but I know that he had an extremely lonely, difficult and uprooted childhood. So he has held on to the value of a degree and still holds on to it as an essential in life. So when in class 11, in my own way, I started showing signs of breaking away from that tradition—that was the next big rift.

Then when I joined NID, they were a bit relieved because it was a five-year professional course. It was under the Ministry of Industry and a sister institute to IIT. It looked like it was a good, proper job-oriented course and that I was on the right path. But then I was chucked out in two years. I did not finish and there was no romantic reason for it. I indulged in a lot of substance and other extra-curricular activities during this time. What happened was that in the two years I had lots of incompletes and I did not feel the urge to drop a semester again and try and complete them as my institute suggested. I said that I would go out and work. So that was the third breakaway.

I came back to Delhi and started looking for work without any educational qualifications outside of a class 12 pass, which I still am. I am not a college graduate. The only reason I have an ECNR (Emigration Check Not Required) stamp on my passport was that my first foreign travel, very early on, was to Dhaka for an advertising agency's copywriting job. The creative director of our agency was a lady, very high up, who knew somebody in the Foreign Ministry. She told them that I had to write a brochure for a client in Bangladesh, and hence needed the ECNR stamp. Ever since, I have the stamp and I am safe. So that is something that made me a legitimate passport holder of India.

Then slowly I started getting advertising jobs and earning money. So my parents relaxed and thought that finally I was doing something with my life. The next break was that I started coming back home very late, like 2 or 3 in the morning, and it was began telling on my parents. So I moved out to preserve my sanity and theirs too. I moved to a typical *barsaati* in Defence Colony. That was a big step but I also knew that my parents were half relieved that at least now I would not bother them by coming home late night. By that time, they were getting used to the idea that there were many breaks yet to come. Then my wife and I were living together for a long time. My parents knew about it but ignored it.

All this came at a point when my parents saw examples of other people following tradition and prospering according to their definition. This created a little sadness in them and a little guilt in me. Now I realize that *Khosla ka Ghosla* was a kind of expiation.

The next break came suddenly while I was doing very well in advertising and earning very good money; within four years I went from a salary of ₹1,200 per month to ₹20,000 per month. So it was a good rise and everybody was very happy. I was one of the upcoming copywriters. I suddenly left it all to start my own filmmaking company with my NID batchmates. That was a complete jump into the unknown. Just when my parents had thought that I was on the road to success, they got this shock. Eventually, that company started doing very well. By that time I had a typical South Delhi house and my parents were very happy about my material wealth. For kids who were barely 28 or 29, we were earning a lot of money those days. We had our own cars and own homes, all this from making ad-films. We were the first batch of filmmakers who were making ad-films out of Delhi including Pradeep Sarkar and Sujit Sarkar. I got married to the same girl whom I had been with for the last seven or eight years. Everything was just fine.

Then the last break came when I left the ad-film company and sold my share to my partner. I started on this extremely stressful 2–3-year-long process of trying to make films where I had just a few of my ad-films and my capital from my past few years of extremely high earning, and my wife who supported me because she was highly qualified. She was an MBA and a highly paid marketing professional. She shared the burden with me. Those two or three years were extremely traumatic because the film was ready but its release was stuck.

The film was made in Delhi. When we decided we were going to make this film and it was all done, I sold my stake to my partner. I knew that making my first feature film while being a full-fledged ad-filmmaker in my current company would not be possible and that my partner would face the unfairness of me not doing anything. So then Jaideep got the producer and me talking. The three of us got together and realized that we gel well, and we see the same product, and so decided to make it.

Preeti: *At that time, were you sure of the kind of market that the movie would have?*

Dibakar: With your first film you do not know anything, you have no idea, and you are naive, arrogant, insecure, impatient, patient—you are a bag full of contrary paradoxes. Worse, if you have not assisted anyone in the craft of film making, all you have are theoretical ideas about feature film making. All I had was practical experience of ad-film making. It kind of passes muster but there is still a lot to do.

The good thing that happened with *Khosla ka Ghosla* was that the film was so tough to make. Therefore, it took so long, the script was written over a long period of time, the shoot finished but after that the edit kept on happening because nobody was picking up the film, so we kept on editing the film on our own, and showing it to people. Ultimately, it reached its final shape. By the time it finally got released, multiplexes had come up and there was a certain kind of domino effect of critical mass that was built up for the film.

Preeti: *So let us re-address the notion of the traditional Indian family set up in* Khosla ka Ghosla *and its ending.*

Dibakar: Coming to the most critical academic question—the ending of the film. I have actually gone on record saying that it is a very regressive ending where you are saying that you are willing to actually overlook your personal focus as a person to give way to that typical *train ka dabba* (box) house where mummy–papa, elder son–younger son all live floor by floor in one joint family heaven. The reason for this is pure commercial expedience. The original ending that I had of *Khosla ka Ghosla* was that Khosla is standing behind his son at the US Embassy trying to get his immigration visa cleared also because Khurana has taken everything and now he has to run away. So Jaideep read it and said it was a very good ending and once you do it you would have sealed your fate as a first-time film maker. Your career will be finished.

Then we came out with another ending, which was aesthetically fulfilling if you take the aesthetics to be dominated by the tone from which the film starts. The tone from which it starts is affection for the family, no doubt about it. You can see that the makers are affectionate towards the father and the son, and though they are showing a fight between them, the makers understand what the father and the son are saying, and they need to come together. You wish that Dashrath and Ram are reunited. That was the tone. If you have started on that tone, the film first and foremost, rather than being a social and polemical exercise, or any other kind of a polemical exercise, is at first an aesthetic exercise. We have to first answer to the aesthetics. If you have set up that tone then you have to end in a tone that completes it. Then aesthetically it is a superior film. Emotionally it drives a stronger point because the tone at which it starts is the tone at which it ends. But that does not mean that I defend the film at all. It is not something I would do again.

Nirmal: *But what is wrong in having that ending. Are we not also husbands and fathers? I am not going away to pick up jobs in places I could get because to me my family matters.*

Dibakar: There is nothing wrong at all. You have enjoyed it sentimentally. I would have done the same. I as a person did not or would not do what Parvin Dabas's character did in the film. I do not stand for what his character does.

Nirmal: *That is fine. You are a filmmaker and you are not writing an autobiography. You are writing for the market.*

Dibakar: Exactly.

Nirmal: *In the end, you are making a movie for the producer and you have a responsibility towards that person as well as the crew. In* Khosla ka Ghosla *— 90% you had your creative satisfaction, you can always give in 10%.*

Dibakar: I agree with you, but within the context of this book and the discussion we are having, I would actually agree with Preeti in saying that if you are discussing the aesthetics of filmmaking, the inner workings and the tradecraft then, just to have a level field of investigation, keep the commercial aspects aside for a while. After all, the commercial aspect never really goes away. If you are adhering to the commercial aspects of filmmaking, then you should also interview David Dhawan, Rohit Shetty and Anees Bazmee. In the field of this fascinating thing that you are trying to do, I would be very open to taking this and ripping this topic apart and seeing where it goes. I would say that *Khosla ka Ghosla*, in truth, for me is a guilt exercise. That is why in the end I go for that sentimental issue of the family coming together.

Having known families, most of us do, we know that there is a side to the family that is diametrically opposed to personal freedom. It is, by definition, designed to create a conflict that defines us as somebody who is a person and somebody who is part of a social unit.

Preeti: *In Jhumpa Lahiri's* Unaccustomed Earth, *Lahiri borrows Nathaniel Hawthorne's quote, 'Human nature will not flourish, any more than a potato, if it be planted and replanted, for too long a series of generations, in the same worn-out soil. My children have had other birthplaces, and, so far as their fortunes may be within my control, shall strike their roots into unaccustomed earth'.*

Dibakar: It depends on what field of sentiments and emotions you are deciding to confine your work into. *Khosla ka*

Ghosla started unapologetically in a tone saying that though this was a dysfunctional family, there is a lot of good here; good people actually conflicting with each other for reasons that are not really meant to hurt each other. They stop fighting when true adversity comes. It is a proverbial, mythical, prodigal-son-returns-home kind of a film. In fact, Anupam Kher and I sat down and realized that *Khosla ka Ghosla* and another commercial film *Ziddi*, which have Sunny Deol and Anupam Kher, have got the same plot. Anupam Kher has an uncontrollable son, they have fights, then one villain comes and the son comes back, fights the villain, saves his father, and Anupam Kher says *mera beta* (my son!). The tone is different. That is all. *Ziddi* was a high-pitched, dramatic, typical overemphasized dialogue *baazi* commercial film, which was very well done. My film is a subtle, detail-oriented, naturalistic exposition but the plot movements, the beginning, the middle and the dénouement are all the same.

So it was a first film, and very luckily, it had enough aesthetics, and enough of a cleverly plotted end, according to our maturity then, and it survived. Probably, today if I were to make *Khosla ka Ghosla* as my fourth film, it will have all of that, will be more mature; probably, the end would still be that the son is going to the US but there is a true rapprochement between them. The father has learned to let the bird fly away. If you love someone, set him/her free. The son is saying I can be abroad and yet I can be home because I have my own family to start with. This is the way of the world. My father will die and I have to live, and tomorrow my son will leave my fold and go. These are some very hard, clear truths of life that you cannot avoid.

When you are making your first film, and you are not so mature, what happens is that you start sugar coating the hard truth, but if you are growing older the right way, then the hard truths do not threaten you anymore. It seems inevitable and somehow you make your peace with it. I have a daughter, and I know at 20 she will tell me,' Listen, my life is my life and you really cannot enter my room without knocking'. I will be hurt, but it is a very comfortable truth you have to live with because that is life.

Life is that once you are born then you die, and that presupposes lots of other truths, which you have to live with. Today, the film would reflect that but at that time it was a function of my maturity.

Now coming to *Oye Lucky! Lucky Oye!* I do not agree with you. Lucky is actually the complete antithesis of Khosla. If you go see the movie again you will see that everything that we hold sacred about the family is broken. The father–son relationship is broken. You can see and understand that the relationship is genuinely attritional and confrontational because of male ego, sexual turf and everything else.

Nirmal: *Do you know of such a family because last night I saw the film and it seemed so real?*

Dibakar: It is nothing new. There are such families all over.

Nirmal: *It is surprising that coming from a Bengali background you have made all your films on Punjabis. You have made very truthful films on Punjabis.*

Dibakar: But I am from Delhi. That is Karol Bagh. I have seen them in front of my eyes. I must say that the immigrant Bengalis living in Delhi live a slightly formaldehyde-preservative life. As any immigrant population anywhere in the world, you have a bunch of outmoded customs and you are trying to keep up with the new milieu where you are living. I cannot make a worthwhile or a truthful film about the Bengali community I have grown up with in

Delhi right now because I cannot find any clear truth about them. It is full of contradictions and adjustments. An immigrant family trying to hold on to the customs of the place it left, while also continuously trying to adapt and be contemporary with the place of its immigration.

Nirmal: *But didn't your first producer expect you to make a Bengali film? Don't they question you? Pradeep Sarkar making a* Parineeta *is fine but Dibakar Banerjee making* Oye Lucky! Lucky Oye!

Dibakar: But *Parineeta* is not a film based on knowledge of detail but a film based on knowledge of literature. It is a film based on the knowledge of perennial and universal human emotions. In *Parineeta* the tradecraft does not rely on the intimate knowledge of detail, usage and expression of human beings. Sarat Chandra's *Parineeta* has been contemporized in terms of outfits, set, etc. to the sixties period, and it works because of its emotional and universal underpinnings of love and family. But my films, by choice, need local detail and observance, and local nuances.

Nirmal: *If I were a producer I would have expected you to make a Bengali film. Was there no pressure on you at all?*

Dibakar: No, no. Anyway, films made in the Hindi language, on Bengalis, don't sell. Also, I do not find it an exciting field of study to actually centre it on. Imagine a film on second-generation Swedish immigrants living in New York and a film on a genuine true-blue Italian family living in an Italian ghetto in New York, which is not a gangster family. You will go for the latter because there is something about the rootedness of culture that gives you ingredients to express things faster. If I have to make a film about Bengali immigrants, I have to first set the context of what there is as the original homeland.

Preeti: *Like* The Namesake.

Dibakar: When you come to *The Namesake*, you realize that you have to be that mature. When I saw Irrfan Khan, I said, Jesus I have Bengali uncles like this, or that I have seen other Bengali professors like this. It was such a scary and true-to-life portraiture. You need to go through all those things to a level where just the plot itself, your knowledge and your maturity of the human condition are enough to tell the story properly. But while I was doing *Oye Lucky! Lucky Oye!* or *Khosla ka Ghosla* I did not have that maturity. I needed the tools, and that would have been the intimate knowledge of behaviour and nuance.

Oye Lucky! Lucky Oye! is distinctly anti-family — whether it is the father–son relationship or the almost incestuous relationship that is about to happen between an adolescent Lucky and the woman who the father gets in his house. Lucky exits from the house and after that his locus is to form his own family in defiance to the family that has rejected him. So when you come to the proverbial brother–brother fight, you see that Lucky is trying to fight for his brother because he thinks this is my family but the brother says, 'Do not come back home'. This is what happens when you go out of the fold — after a while you come back and expect to be welcomed. But the family says that now we are a family and you are an outsider. Then he tells his brother that he would get married in a five-star hotel and that then they would come. He tries to bribe his family to come for his marriage. So, because he is a very confused and misguided person he is trying to rediscover the family that he never had. Of course, that does not mean that the family is waiting there to say 'Oooh! We are all together'.

Oye Lucky! Lucky Oye! is a direct antithesis of *Khosla ka Ghosla*. The latter is, of course, the pillar of all middle-class values. Lucky, actually, in every scene is anti-middle class including the scene where the adolescent Lucky and his friends are beating up that public school guy, which is actually me. I was beaten up by the government school guys as a kid, so it was an anti-autobiography! If you see from Lucky's point of view, he is the class enemy. Throughout when you see Dr Handa, you experience the quintessence of the genteel Delhi middle-class, club-going, respectability. Doctor no less, but then you realize he is a veterinarian. Handa's line when Lucky asks him whether he is a *kutton ka doctor* (doctor for dogs) is—my father pulled my ears and made me sit for the exam. This one line is his own youthful regret.

Ultimately, you see it is Handa who is the actual *gunda*. He is the guy who is absolutely the typical villain. Lucky says, 'I have to slap you'. That is the last stance of the defeated class. Either slap someone or go see an Amitabh Bachchan movie and yell, yes we will win! So definitely, it is anti-middle class, anti-family and dystopian.

I went more dystopian in my second film and took a huge risk by writing a script that was not narrative but was episodic. I merged realities, where it starts with a TV interview and ends with a TV interview—it encapsulates the whole film as if you were seeing a five-minute criminal segment. Then you try and cast Paresh Rawal in three roles and put them together. Just a mythical way of saying that the guy that betrays is always the father figure. First the real father, then Goga *bhai* who is the criminal father figure and then Handa who is the ultimate father figure.

Nirmal: *Is there a certain amount of glamorization of crime and negativity in your films?*

Dibakar: No. I will start my answer in a very oblique manner. There is a practice in Indian films that an actor comes and you ask him what role he is doing in a film. He would say that in this film he plays the character of a doctor or that he plays a character who is an engineer. You laugh. There is no character called a doctor or an engineer. Similarly for me or any self-respecting creative person who is indulging in narrative arts or literature, there is no negative and there is no positive. There is no hero or villain in the social, moral and ethical context. A hero is only defined as the person from whose point of view you choose to tell the story. There could be another film that could take Khurana's (*Khosla ka Ghosla*) life as centre stage and tell Boman's story.

The hero is an arbitrary choice impressed by the writer or maker onto the fabric of the narrative. He can choose Rama or Ravana to be the hero. Then the villain is defined by virtue of the hero who stands in the way of the hero's dramatic quest. This is basic, aesthetic stuff so I am not saying anything new. But when you realize it for yourself, it definitely has an importance. Therefore, I have no special like or dislike for any positivity or negativity as shown by the profession of the characters. A land shark who usurps other people's land, the character has to be interesting for me, and I do not want to demonize him. I would rather demonize the process. If you see *Khosla ka Ghosla* the process is thoroughly demonized. Your sympathy lies with Anupam Kher's character and you see the troubles he is going through and the sympathetic treatment tells you that what is happening to this character is wrong. Therefore, in the end, when he fools Khurana, by using the same process, giving him the money back, we all cheer for him.

Nirmal: *How does Khurana get so easily fooled?*

Dibakar: Precisely. Because he is a lovable character. He gets fooled because of Sethi. What the film is also talking about is that every villain has a super *baap* (super boss). When they place Sethi in front of Khurana, in every frame,

Khurana is looking at Sethi with reverence. One day Sethi comes in shorts, the next day Khurana copies him. This is to repeatedly emphasize the fact that Khurana actually wants to be Sethi where you empathize with him, and that is why he is fooled. But the fact is that in the overall construct of the film you see that since the process is demonized, there is no doubt in the maker's mind that what is happening to an honest, tax-paying middle-class guy is wrong.

What is happening in *Oye Lucky! Lucky Oye!* is mapping a grey story. As an arbitrary choice, when we decide to follow the locus of Lucky the thief as the hero, then you have to define everything that comes in the face of Lucky — the anti-hero. Every policeman, every person who stops Lucky from stealing or pushes him towards stealing is a villain. But even then you see the fabric of the story, when you see that the maker goes into showing what Lucky went through as a kid — his father gets another woman in the house, that woman actually makes a pass at Lucky — this kind of a confused childhood where you have no sense of protection from anywhere. Your father could beat you to pulp or your father's mistress could fondle you. At the same time when you go out on the road you have to fight with other kids to survive. There is absolutely no sense of protection. This guy knows that unless and until he fights back or picks up something and runs, he does not stand for anything. Ultimately, you are making the same clichéd statement that it is the circumstances that make a person a criminal and that there is nothing genetic about it. How you define a criminal is also a major factor in deciding whether the guy is a criminal or not. You see the locus of the guy, and then you see that the process is demonizing him. Then comes the pressure of the 50 minutes of fame. You see Lucky repeatedly trying to become a big guy, as somebody to contend within society, and his relation with

Handa is the same relationship that Khurana had with Sethi. He starts fraternizing with Handa with a very clear aim—now I will make myself genteel and respectable, I will now speak in English, I will now go to a club too.

Nirmal: *Because he was in love by then.*

Dibakar: His love is that he has a woman to take care of. He is fitting in check boxes. I have a girlfriend—check. I have a genteel family to go to—check. I have a club membership—check. Also, I have a portrait of my parents in my bedroom and they need not be my parents—they can be something I stole. He is stealing himself a life. When he goes to his girlfriend's house, his girlfriend's mother asks him to get a toaster, so in a way he is buying relationships. But also, it shows that the guy himself is being as much used by society as he is using it, and as much violence, and criminal activity is being done to him as he is doing to others. So I do not think there is any glorification of crime.

Preeti: *Many reviews talk about the fact that while* LSD: Love, Sex Aur Dhokha *is a critique of voyeurism at a certain level, just as* Oye Lucky! Lucky Oye! *is a critique of a consumerist society, in a way, you are also using the same ethos to sell the films. As a filmmaker, do you think, the onus lies with you, to make certain kind of movies? Is film as art just pure aesthetics or do you think you have a larger responsibility/role?*

Dibakar: You have mixed two or three very heavy metaphors together.

One is, what you said, that when you are making a film that is critiquing a certain aspect of society, could you propagate it and market it by taking advantage of the same ideology. The answer to that is yes, probably morally, and aesthetically a bit indefensible—morals I do not believe in—but I would rather say that a film that expresses my anger and displeasure at the way my society is behaving is seen by as many people as possible. It makes it even more my responsibility to make sure as a producer/director (as I was of *LSD: Love, Sex Aur Dhokha*) that what I have made reaches others. To take a rough example, if a social activist wants to get his message across, probably he will think of a catchy headline or poster and get a public relation (PR) firm or political party to endorse that subject, to come to the stage and vocalize that to society. Then it remains upon him to see that his message and his means remain as undiluted as ever.

The second question was regarding my responsibility towards my art. Of course, every artist has a responsibility like every human has a responsibility. A history professor's responsibility is to teach history, to teach historical perspective and to teach what the need for history is. But what is true history and what history he will propound to his students is his personal choice. You can definitely question my view of how I look at society. I have the responsibility to present what I think is the truth. Often what happens is that it is not very subjective. When you see my film and when you see a typical revenge saga, you will want to speak to me as a thinking person rather than the maker of that revenge saga. This shows that at least in the treatment and the intention of my film, I am trying to be as honest and truthful as I can be under the human condition. After that I have no other responsibility.

If you say that I have shown sex in my film, the first thing is that when you notice *LSD: Love, Sex Aur Dhokha* you realize that the most unattractive and cringing part of the film is sex. That is the core of the primary need from which I have made the film. The core was that I have always seen the act of sex in a film, most of the time, as a blind spot where in addition to having lots of interactions between people, suddenly the act of sex becomes the act of sex and nothing else. Then you start packaging it through lighting, though slow motion, through music, through the expression of ecstasy frequently on the heroine's face because it is a male-dominated medium (the act of sex is always seen through the woman's body — through the pleasure that the woman is getting while the man's pleasure is a token thing). I find such a portrayal of the act of sex very boring. It is like a shot of a man eating. But if a short sequence of a man eating gives you the pre-knowledge that his *dal* is poisoned, and the man does not know it, you know it, and now the man eats, and while he is eating he is talking about what he is going to do tomorrow, that is, the true aesthetic purpose of the shot of a man eating — it becomes a tool of storytelling. Every mouthful that he takes is a moment of reckoning for you. When will he die? When? Plus, he is talking about

Source: Authors.

tomorrow. So everything points to that moment—it talks about life, it talks about impending death and it talks of the helplessness of man against death, etc.

Similarly, can we have sex scenes that show something else? For example, there are two sex scenes in Bertolucci's *Last Tango in Paris*. One is when Marlon Brando and Maria meet for the first time in an apartment. The other scene is when Marlon almost forces sex on her even while they have been living together for a while. You realize these two characters are using sex as a way to use each other, dominate each other till the girl says no more and she shoots him. She has already figured out an alibi for the police—he tried to rape me. She decides that she will live by the truth and not use sex to use somebody or be used. That kind of sex is fascinating, which is why we have the central sex scene in *LSD: Love, Sex Aur Dhokha*. I was extremely vindicated when in the small towns where it had been publicized only on the virtue of the sex scene, the film was booed, and people walked out cursing the film and deriding it for having nothing sleazy.

Nirmal: You consciously used the medium in a different way, like the different camera format, to shoot the sex scene. How did your producer allow such a scene?

Dibakar: Absolutely. The medium is the message in a way. Plus, it was inherent in the narration. If you want to make a found footage film, the story has to be told by simulating the accidents of the footage that has been lost or of the footage that is there with you. The shooting and the visual composition have to simulate the accidentality of the camera as well as the known accidentality of the camera.

For example, in the first story there are parts where Rahul, the filmmaker, is actually trying to make Aditya Chopra-esque kind of romance with a small digital video camera and it is the most clichéd composition you can ever think of. But there are other parts where he is trying to film the making of the film or he is just actually obsessed with the camera and the girl, and often the camera is not shooting something but you can hear something. So by the accident of the juxtaposition of an image and a sound that do not necessarily go together, you create dramatic tension, and therefore, dramatic interest in the scene. So we had to simulate that because found footage needs to have that. So we had to invent techniques to do that. We had to figure out ways of attaching the camera to the actor's body so that he could act and shoot at the same time. We had to find ways of choreographing the cameraman's and the actor's movements so the cameraman would place the camera here and move with the actor so that it simulates the actor's point of view yet the actor is not burdened with the handling of the camera.

The second story was completely opposite to the first one. It had static cameras at a distance. A primal rule of filmmaking says that when you want the audience to feel what the character is feeling, you have to go as close to the character as possible. When you have to show a grand thing you have to go as far away as possible. But by virtue of putting a camera 10 feet away from a hero as he is crying or as he is professing his love, and at the same time wanting the scene to be emotionally charged without breaking the rules that you have imposed on yourself, takes a lot of planning. The story and the writing had to be done with that in mind. So the screenplay had to solve all these problems in the writing of it where this girl and boy are kissing but the camera is up there. So you have to devise the scene, the edit, the dialogue and the action in such a way that you stick to the rule of the game that you have made for yourself without affecting the emotional charge of the film. Therefore, the narrative matters. The camera does not move. The actors come into the frame; it is like a stage. The story, which had security cameras in it, was almost written like a stage play with very careful breaking of the rules. For example, at one point we needed to go very close to the guy's face. So the premise that we invented was that the camera is in maintenance. That is why you can see his face close-up. Then he can see the girl's face in the monitor where he zooms in—that is why you can see her close-up. So the formation of the rule and the breaking of it were done as a balance between what you need to tell and the rigour of how you need to tell it. The minute you cheat with your own brief, you can see a flaccid narrative coming out. But when you don't cheat with your own brief, it does not happen, no matter how long, pedantic or how interesting the product is. So we had to embed the logic of shooting of the film into the script.

Nirmal: But didn't it take a lot of convincing for the producer to let you do this kind of script and camerawork?

Dibakar: It was a very cheap film. It was a very safe film. Ekta Kapoor knew that the moment you have a film called *LSD: Love, Sex Aur Dhokha*, with me directing it, there would be audience interest. She is a very intelligent and, in some ways, courageous producer.

Nirmal: Ekta Kapoor was making saas–bahu serials and you gave her a complete makeover. Why did you choose her as a producer?

Dibakar: They came to me. They thought that I wanted to make a big, commercial film. I know it because later on Ekta told me so. She heard the narration and said that it was really interesting, and then when she heard the cost her financial advisor must have told her that even if no one watched the film, it would still work out, plus because this was a new, interesting product, they thought it would be a very good rub off because this was the first new film that the new avatar of her company was producing. Even then she was very conscious of it as the makeover. Now we are talking about it as a postscript. She was so intelligent that she realized that if this product was done truthfully, and then marketed well, it would be a makeover for her company's image.

The way we survive is to do things that we want to do by being extremely cheap about it, and not take the personal sacrifices that we make as sacrifices. I do not have a very expensive car. I have a normally expensive car by Indian middle-class standards. It pays off in the end and that is why you have the independence to do what you want to do.

The same goes with *Shanghai*.

Nirmal: Shanghai *is the most expensive film you have made till now.*

Dibakar: This film by its premise needed to show the scale and the vibe of a small Indian town gearing up for a political and financial makeover. If you live in a small town you will know how momentous it can be in that place's history. Imagine Delhi before the Asiad or imagine it before the Commonwealth Games. We needed a scale that required a certain budget. Please do not be misguided by the publicity. The publicity of the film gives the impression that it's a huge film. It is not that huge; again, it is a very safe bet for a producer to the extent that he knew that having made the film we will probably make profit on the table right now even before releasing it. This is a contingent issue in how you make films and how you promote them. I would rather be a smart producer who will make his film at the cheapest possible cost and I would rather put my skills into making that film achieve the biggest bang for the buck.

As a producer, I have the confidence to say that the one rupee that I spent on a film will look about three times more expensive than the one rupee that another director will put on the film. Then what you do is that when you make the film you try and make it look bigger because you're not only advertising for the audience, you're also advertising for the trade. Herein comes the ultimate corruption of the audience. Today as an audience you are aware that this film is commercial, or that this film is big, or that this film is small—this was never supposed to be. The audience is sensitized to a film being a big film, or a commercial film, or a glam film, or an independent film. The audience is being bombarded by the value of the film not in terms of the story that it tells but by the attendant paraphernalia of the film. The attendant publicity of the film tells the audience that you should see this film because it is a 400-million film and after the release weekend the advertising comes up and tells you that you should see this film because this is a 1,100-million first-weekend film. The logic being that you are a fool if you miss this film that everyone else is going to watch.

It is the same thing as saying that 78% people prefer Colin to Rin as their preferred washing agent. Then there is a scientist who says that research has proven that 78% of families use Colin rather than Rin. So it is exactly that kind of consumer advertising. You are being bombarded by a pure consumer-driven publicity exercise. I know that if I convince you that I am a big filmmaker you will come and see my films, and not because I am a filmmaker that you like. My mother has seen many films because she feels compelled to like them and when I ask her what is it that she liked, she cannot mention a single thing. Now she has stopped going to watch films under the pressure to like a film because of its size, budget, star cast or myth propagation around a director.

Nirmal: Did you have more freedom when you were making Khosla ka Ghosla *or are you too compelled by your brand value?*

Dibakar: It is the same for me. My brand value is something that I impose upon you for you to pay money to see my films. If I use my brand value to fetter myself, then it is a stupid brand. The only thing that constraints you is the budget, believe me.

Nirmal: But now you can go to a big star and they will want to work with you.

Dibakar: I will give you the formula to that. Today a big star will want to work with me. Now there are two ways — either I can hobble my freedom or not hobble it. The way I will hobble it is if a star comes to me and says that this is my script and I think that with this star's name and my reputation, I can easily make this much money. The moment I let him take the lead and the moment I give him the decision power to come in on his terms, I have lost my freedom. I may have earned a lot more money but I have lost my freedom. The way I would work in a situation like this is that I would tell the star, 'Sir, here is the story, it is alternative cinema, and what I can do for you is that instead of making it in 400 million, which is the normal budget for any film of yours, I will make it within 200 million. You will face no risk because your name will fetch this many millions in the opening week itself. Apart from that, I will do this and this for you in the film but the rest will be up to me and you cannot interfere with that'. Believe me, this is the way *Khosla ka Ghosla, Oye Lucky! Lucky Oye!, LSD: Love, Sex Aur Dhokha* and *Shanghai* were made.

When I speak to a newspaper, I say *Shanghai* is a big film, that I put all my strength into it and that there is an item number—all this is part of the publicity for the film. The truth is that we have made *Shanghai* at a price that no other Bollywood director/producer could make. Today we are projecting it as a big film so that we can maximize the profit and then go onto another film of the same type, which costs 20-30% less than the average Bollywood cousin of that stature and yet gives an impression that it is as big or probably bigger.

Nirmal: Take a bigger star.

Dibakar: Even if I take a bigger star I would like to make the film with that star for 20-30% less money than the industry standard of what you get for that star as a film budget.

Nirmal: Don't you have anything against the star system as such?

Dibakar: The star system has got nothing to do with film-making. The star system has got to do with the society that it belongs to. You have various grades of society. A simple comparison is that stars would be a little less potent in Europe than stars would be in a country like India. Europe probably has a tradition of individualism, and therefore, a star as a role model to follow and blindly ape is less potent in such an individualistic society.

Ours is a hugely unjust, imbalanced society, where there is tremendous poverty and there is tremendous control by a very small minority over a huge majority through power; business and money; through political laws and formulations that are more about sustenance of the rich than about an equitable distribution of wealth; it is a colonial system. It is just that our re-hauling has not been a clear one. The colonizers had to make money. A forest officer's main role was to see to it that wood logging was done according to the correct financial practices, and his main job was to harness the logging wealth of the forest. His main job was not to take care of the animals and people who lived in the forest. In a society where the minority rules either through propaganda, economic and legal systems, or through tradition, and uses the large majority for economic and social means, a star system is the quickest way to achieve that. The star system exists not only in Bollywood but also in politics, the other great motivator.

Preeti: *So can a filmmaker like you survive in an industry like this without on the sheer merit of contact?*

Dibakar: You survive marginally and you might as a choice want to stay on the margin because there your voice will forever be a voice of dissent and a voice of the alternative. Three hundred million people will not see it but the 100 thousand people who do see it will be forever emboldened to do something else and that will take the movement forward. So my decision to work or not work with a star will depend on my decision of how marginal I would like to get because a star system is not a criminal system foisted on somebody by somebody. We deserve the society that we get.

We have huge numbers of a traditional mass of people who still have not acquired the habit of thinking anything out for themselves. It is not a moral judgement; it is just the way things are. We define ourselves by tradition, and we do not define ourselves by what we like or what we want to do. Therefore, a star system is the quickest way to tell the audience that look this 6-feet tall, fair-skinned man with six pack abs. He is the ideal of male beauty and character and moral duty, and you should follow this guy. Of course, you are dark skinned, you are skinny because you are not well-fed and do not have time to work out but as long as you aspire to be this person, you are fine.

Preeti: *So if you want to come into the mainstream and, as a conscious choice, do not want to remain on the fringe any longer, and are not antagonistic to the idea of the star system, would it in sometime start dictating your content?*

Dibakar: There are two ways to survive—either you get subverted or you will subvert.

Preeti: *Could a subject like* LSD: Love, Sex Aur Dhokha *be made with stars?*

Dibakar: No. Therefore, *LSD: Love, Sex Aur Dhokha* budget has to be this much; therefore *LSD: Love, Sex Aur Dhokha* technique and the way you make it is this much—it defines itself. The creative premise says that the moment you see known faces you will not take it as found footage. It will no longer be gory, visceral or that scary. But, by not having stars you will know that you will confine your film to a 100 million kind of final figure and you are fine with that because the film costs 20 million to make. It is a question of you knowing that this story needs scale and money, so you need one star who will carry the movie. Then you go to the star and tell him what it is like, and through your creative brand you tell the star that the film will be made according to your wishes rather than the star's wishes. The star says no, you walk away and you do not make that film. The star says yes, and you make the film. It is as simple as that.

The trick is to go on making what you want to, year after year, and that itself gives you kinetic energy and a kind of standing. Ultimately, some people will say that he knows something we do not, so let us trust him and do this film. That is the final call when they say that as long as you are there we can do this film. It is as simple as that. It can get complex if you let it get so. That does not mean that I have not made any mistakes. I have made huge mistakes but as long as you learn from them, it is fine.

Preeti: *In terms of the narrative, these days we see a lot of stories about multiple characters, episodic in structure but somehow linked through the cityscape.* Life in a Metro *would be an example, or to an extent* LSD: Love, Sex Aur Dhokha. *What is it within that concept that allows for greater creativity? Why are so many filmmakers experimenting with this format?*

Dibakar: In *LSD: Love, Sex Aur Dhokha*, I claim a much bigger connection between the three stories, the way we played with time, and cause and effect, and the fundamental rule that every story has a beginning, a middle and an end, not necessarily in that order. We made it all topsy-turvy and we joined the three stories in time. That I think was very ingenious. It was the most attractive aspect for me, as a tradesperson of films where my tools are time. What is narration if not events in time! So I actually take a fundamental aspect of my structure, that is, time, and manipulate it in a way which is very new and very satisfying. It is like saying that I can take wood and now melt it and mould it into a sign or a shape, which is exactly what they do with a particle board. That is why we have those woody looking chairs, which are yet shaped like plastic or steel.

When you explain *LSD: Love, Sex Aur Dhokha* in terms of tradecraft, how we put the same old material and applied a new scientific process to it (well, nothing is new, a lot of people have also done it, and I am talking about it within the confine of our historical and social perspective) and that we took it and we changed the material, and we made wood behave like metal, that to me is a very interesting exercise. I would like to claim that distinction for *LSD: Love, Sex Aur Dhokha*.

As Dibakar finished, his long-time associate Kanu Behl, who co-wrote *LSD: Love, Sex Aur Dhokha* and will be making his directorial debut with *Titli* soon, chipped in. Dibakar nodded approvingly to his replies.

Kanu Behl: I agree with Dibakar on this. *LSD: Love, Sex Aur Dhokha* does not fit into the bracket of a multiple-track film trying to deal with the confusion of the city. But I can totally see where those kinds of narratives are coming from because the filmmakers that are coming up are most obsessed about those ideas. We do not have a strong supply line of directors or writers coming in from the interiors of India, from small towns or from villages. Most writers and filmmakers are city-bred, and their conflicts and ideas have to do with narratives that are present in the city. That is how there is this new movement of fractured narratives and three stories linking together. It is almost like trying to make sense of the world around you and this new shift in B-town culture where there are no joint families anymore and there are single household units everywhere. So you are suddenly staring at a row of flats with 20 windows instead of a big house with five rooms and 20 people, looking and wondering what is happening in all of those 20 windows. So that one whole big life of 20 people in one house is fractured into 20 lives that you are trying to make sense of.

Preeti: *But why now, why at this point of time? Nuclear families have been there for a while.*

Kanu Behl: Well, I think it also coincides with a change in the way we look at films. All of it is linked. The way our society has changed, we have opened up, money is coming through different sources into filmmaking, and studios are more corporatized, and the flow of money coming in is different. All that impacts the kind of conditions that are getting set up for the sort of narratives that are being written.

Preeti: *Do you think there is a greater amount of professionalism and transparency in the industry? As an insider, how do you feel the industry has evolved over the last five years?*

Kanu Behl: I would say there is a greater degree of transparency, although I have not been that long in Mumbai. Amongst my age group people, we hear stories of what it used to be like, but ever since I have been here it seems different from what it was earlier. Definitely, there are greater chances to make the films that young filmmakers really want to make rather than pander to a star or a producer wanting to make a certain kind of film.

Kiran Rao

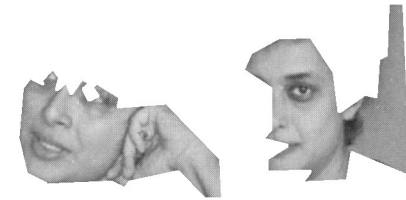

Courtesy: Kiran Rao.

Independent filmmaker and screenwriter, Kiran Rao, born to a Kannadiga Brahmin father and a Saraswat Brahmin mother from Karnataka, a standard middle-class family, spent her childhood and a considerable chunk of her teenage years in the city of Calcutta. She went to Loreto House and then to La Martiniere School. She is married to Bollywood superstar Aamir Khan, and they have a son named Azad.

Rao's earliest recollections comprise books from the local library, Carnatic music, films on Doordarshan and English musicals such as *The Sound of Music* and *My Fair Lady*. From Calcutta, Rao left for Mumbai where she majored in Economics as part of her Bachelor's degree but quickly realized that her heart was set on the visual and performing arts. Ambivalent regarding the exact choice of subject she decided to attend the AJK Mass Communication Research Centre at Jamia Millia Islamia in Delhi where she familiarized herself with the principal elements of electronic media and film.

Never an ardent movie watcher, Rao had always been a music junkie, a devourer of literature and photography, and a promising writer. It did not take her long to recognize that the business of filmmaking would bring together and gratify all her lifelong passions. After a brief stint in the advertising world, her ideals got the better of her, and Rao set out to make her mark in Indian cinema. From the very beginning, she was convinced that her films would bear no resemblance to mainstream Bollywood fare, but the valiant amateur understood that she would have to learn the ropes on a Hindi film set.

Rao's schooling began as a third assistant director (AD) on the set of the critically acclaimed Aamir Khan starrer *Lagaan* (2001) directed by Ashutosh Gowariker. Working on the period film, in physically trying desert conditions, with a legion of actors was no mean feat, but Rao lapped up the lessons on filmmaking. She went on to act as a second AD in Mira Nair's independent film *Monsoon Wedding* (2001). Later, she assisted Ashutosh Gowariker, again, in *Swades* (2004).

Kiran began writing the script for her debut film *Dhobi Ghat* (*Mumbai Diaries*) in 2005. It took her almost three years to complete the script and achieve a sense of satisfaction. Eventually, the film was released in 2011 under the banner of Aamir Khan's home production. Screened at the Toronto International Film Festival and the London Film Festival, *Dhobi Ghat* gathered critical praise for its melancholic portrayal of Mumbai, sensitive to its hues and moods, and for the overlapping stories of love and loss.

As the director of the film herself concedes, *Dhobi Ghat* is a definitive ode to the city of Mumbai. Rao claims that while other authentic depictions of Mumbai have been achieved in films of the past, there was almost always only one aspect of the city being dealt with. In her own film she has tried to capture the layered experience of living in a versatile space, such as Mumbai, which melts social and economic divisions even as it upholds them. Rao differentiates between someone who has maybe grown up in Mumbai and someone who comes to the city and finds her way. She, of course, is the latter inhabitant.

Dhobi Ghat weaves a non-linear plot of intersecting lives, in the process highlighting the heterogeneity of different people and their experiences in Mumbai. It brings to the fore characters belonging to different economic classes and their mundane interactions with each other. The shy Salman Khan who worships Munna (Prateik Babbar) is a *dhobi* (washerman) by day and a rat killer by night. We see a latent romance, albeit a one-sided one, between this young working-class man and one of his clients, Shai (Monica Dogra). This non-resident, Wall Street banker, is on an indefinite 'break' from work and roams the city with Munna, armed with her camera and its outsider lens. Shai, in turn, is infatuated with the gloomy artist, Arun (Aamir Khan), who prefers a solitary, exclusive relationship with his canvas, until he discovers the video diary of an unhappily married woman, Yasmin (Kriti Malhotra). Rao's love for the visual arts comes through as the characters in her film discover each other, and their own selves, through the medium of the visual, be it a camera lens, a video diary or a painting.

This honest affection for the arts has translated into an attempt to encourage non-traditional cinema in India, and Rao is unequivocal in her support of alternative cinema. Most recently, Kiran has taken it upon herself to present Anand Gandhi's masterpiece, *Ship of Theseus* (2013), successfully getting a limited theatrical release for it in multiplexes. Though she has no financial stake in the film, she feels that avant-garde cinema must get a chance to reach its target audience without having to compete with big-budget films. Rao's dream is to create a space where alternative cinema can be nurtured and, more importantly, reach its viewers.

The Personal as the Voyeur—
The Aesthetics of Meaning

Preeti: *Let's start with where you come from, your childhood and your growing-up years.*

Kiran: My parents are from South India. My dad is from Mysore and my mother is technically from South Kanara, part of this small community called the Chitrapur Saraswats, and she's grown up all over the country, mostly in North India, in UP. For both of them this was a second marriage. They are both Brahmins, but she is a Saraswat Brahmin and he is a Kannadiga Brahmin. They are both from Karnataka, but they speak different languages and come from completely different cultures. My mother speaks Konkani. Their food habits are very different. Their traditions are quite nuanced. It's a very small but interesting community. My father is a proper Kannadiga Brahmin who grew up with a whole lot of siblings in Mysore and came to Calcutta to study for his Bachelor's—went to Calcutta University. He stayed on there and worked with Williams, which was a British steel company.

My father's first spouse died and my mother's first spouse died, and they both had children from their first marriages, one daughter each. And their next—their collaboration—produced me.

Preeti: *What were the circumstances of their meeting? Was it arranged?*

Kiran: Yeah, it was kind of arranged. My father's uncle knew my maternal grandfather very well. They were good friends. He was the one who suggested that they meet. A sort of a holiday was engineered, where my grand uncle used to live, I think in Coimbatore or somewhere. That's where they met and then kept in touch through letters over several months. They decided to marry, and literally, less than 11 months later, I was born. I was born in Bangalore. My father lived in Calcutta at that time. So my first 18 years were spent in Calcutta. I actually consider myself Bengali more than anything else. I went to Bangalore for holidays with my grandmum and I visited Mysore on an occasion, but my roots are really in Calcutta. I'm really grateful for that. It was just about the most wonderful place to be growing up in. We had no notion at all of money, class, none of that. My father was a regular middle-class employee, but we always grew up with the idea that we could enjoy ourselves without much money. We went to a very good school, and we always had books, no toys; I don't remember toys very much. But books and music, and luckily for us, thanks to the company, we had membership to a club so there was a library, which was much used by all of us, and a pool and tennis. So my childhood years were really blissful and I enjoyed it.

Preeti: *How was your equation with your siblings?*

Kiran: It was very good. One of my sisters grew up with me, while the other grew up with an uncle of mine. She is eight-and-a-half years older than me. She had to endure me in my precocious childhood when I wanted to be part of every game. She was really a very sweet and gentle elder sister. After a point, she left home and I was much younger, and there's a big gap in many ways in keeping in touch. My formative years, in my teens, she had already left to work—so we lost touch a little bit later, but when we were younger, we were very close and I relied on her a lot.

I loved school. I went to Loreto House. It was literally five minutes from my house. We lived in Central Calcutta. So, when I think about it now, I had quite a luxurious life, even though we didn't have too much money. We lived in the centre of town. Everything was a short walk away. We went to school by a handcart rickshaw, even though it was so close. We had a club close by. So I don't know that much about the rest of Calcutta except the market we used to go to—Park Circus market, Ballygunge Circular Road where we had friends. My memories of Calcutta are of that little square area around Park Street, Camac Street and Wood Street. I really loved Calcutta.

I loved the completely carefree, not bothered by anything kind of upbringing that we had. Our parents did let us know that we couldn't afford stuff and that was fine, but that didn't mean that we couldn't have a grand time without it and we did.

Preeti: *What was the culture like at home? Did movies have a greater role than literature? What about outdoor activities?*

Kiran: We weren't into films at all. My father used to be very much into films when he was in school and right through college. In fact, he used to collect those sorts of handouts; I forget what they're called, small posters that they used to give because those days the films were run by MGM and Warner—so actually the studios used to be here. I have the whole collection of all the films he used to watch, and he literally went every single week that there was a new release, Friday of whichever week. He was a big film buff. I don't think my mum was. But that didn't sort of translate to us at all, and by the time we were growing up, in the seventies, I don't think films were very conducive for children to watch. They were very violent and my parents just didn't think them good enough for us to watch. We used to watch the films that came on Sundays on Doordarshan. That was my exposure to cinema.

I never remember being super excited about movies when I was young. What we did get excited by though were the screenings at our club, on Friday nights, either in a big hall or out in the open. It wasn't a film necessarily playing in the cinema. It could be *Sholay*, or it could be whatever was playing at the time. My film theatre experience was at the club. I never went to a cinema hall. I remember going once for *The Sound of Music*, and thereafter I went in my teens. So that club theatre experience was fantastic because it was very homely; it was lights dimmed and a huge screen—a proper theatre experience for me.

Preeti: *What about theatre?*

Kiran: Yes, plays, sometimes too—on occasion. We were taken to see theatre whenever there was something that my parents thought was nice, such as a musical. We had a record player and we listened to music a lot. My maternal grandfather was very much into music. They had quite a few old musicals because their family used to love singing. So I remember growing up to *My Fair Lady* and *Camelot*, and some amount of South Indian Carnatic classical music.

The club was free, you see, anyone could come and watch the film. Of course, during the interval you signed up for snacks. The parents would sit and have their beer while the children watched the film. It was a nice family experience. Though I loved going to the club to watch films, but I don't ever remember... you know I hear stories of people being obsessed with films—wanting to go to the cinema and watching films, but that wasn't me. Even today I rush out to the see the films that I really want, but I'm not the kind who has to see every film that comes or that I can't do without watching a film — weeks and months go by without my watching a film. I'm actually much more of a music and book person than a movie person, but I love photographs. If there's anything that I'm much more a buff of, it's photography. I love looking at pictures. How I arrived at films was also through photography.

Nirmal: *You mentioned being surrounded by books — so you read a lot of books.*

Kiran: I read a lot and we had access to the club library, which was very well stocked. In those days there was hardly any Indian literature to read, so I've had what I consider a very colonial upbringing. We had mostly British writers, some American writers and some European writers. At school we had Irish nuns. So my whole association with language is very colonial. I loved to read then and I love to read now. Maybe I didn't read as much as my sister. My sister was so obsessive about reading, even when she was eating she would read the writing on the cornflakes *dabba*.

Preeti: *Who were your favourite authors?*

Kiran: Of course, having gone through the Enid Blyton stage — that passed by — and then *Anne of Green Gables* and stuff like that. One of the books that I remember making a great impression on me because I read it quite young, I must have read it in my early teens, was *Lord of the Rings*. I really enjoyed it — it was such a cinematic book also, full of images and adventure, and so much darkness and intrigue. That's one of the books that I recall the experience of reading. I used to enjoy reading fantasy quite a lot. Other than that, writers like Somerset Maugham, Wodehouse, Nevil Shute—my mother was a big fan of Nevil Shute. I don't remember offhand because the library had so many books.

It used to be most exciting because they were all hardbound and you would go along these big shelves, and search for 'M', and find a Marquez book. You never could see the cover, so I don't remember books by their cover because they were all standardized, bound books. Then they had the children's library section, which they made slightly later on, where I spent endless afternoons because they were stocked in comic books such as *Asterix*, *Tintin*, *Lucky Luke*—a whole bunch of these. I was obsessed with *Asterix*, obsessed in the sense that at one stage I could tell you who were the characters from which book, everything. Even now I can to some extent. *Asterix* was a big thing in our home. Whenever our father went on tour, he would bring a comic. He went on tour a lot because he worked in marketing and he was out for 15 days of the month. That was the thing we waited for the most: the new *Asterix and Cleopatra*. Now when I read them I just go into their world. In those days you're in such a hurry to soak it up, and then you read them a second and third time, and I must be reading it the 150th time and you still see something that you didn't see. It is phenomenal.

Nirmal: *You were fortunate to be in Calcutta where there was a reading habit. I teach in Delhi University, and in Delhi it's very bad. I have two, almost grown-up children, but they just don't read.*

Kiran: I think may be our generation didn't have the option of TV, computers, internet and video games. We never had video games in Calcutta. I think children in Bombay did have them. We had music. I learned piano and went to the Calcutta School of Music. I don't think that

I'd ever want to work in music, but a project that associates music with writing would excite me the most. I would enjoy that. Music is something that connects most viscerally with me.

Nirmal: *Why wasn't your first film a musical?*

Kiran: I don't know if I'll ever be able to make a musical. Actually, music is a very personal thing for me. It's a journey that I'm going through all the time. It's one part of me that's an island—music is my little island. I get onto it whenever I don't want anyone else to come into that space. It's when I'm most with myself. So I'm into music, in the sense of, not putting it out there so much. It's soaking it up that I prefer. I love Hindustani classical. It's all these images, visuals, moods that just influence me when I listen to music.

Nirmal: *You had a Carnatic music background, your parents are from Karnataka and you grew up in Bengal. How were you introduced to Hindustani classical music?*

Kiran: We listened to a lot of Hindustani as well. Earlier, I said Carnatic because almost every Sunday, my father would put on *Suprabhatam* by M.S. Subbalakshmi and my clearest memories are of that. Slightly later, I was introduced to Doraiswamy Iyengar's veena. But Hindustani classical also played in my house. My mother was very keen that I should sing. I used to sing quite well so my mother tried to send me to learn Hindustani. My aunts, and a lot of people I know, are in music. The teacher was an enormous fat lady who put the harmonium on her lap as if it was a small accordion, and she scared the hell out of me. It was on her lap, on one large thigh and it had nothing to do with what I loved about music. It was horrible, and I said that I couldn't do this. But the love was there even then.

What I like the most about Carnatic music was its percussiveness. But what I love about Hindustani, and it's my first love, is complete abandon. You can't sing with any formula, or any prescribed sense... you don't know what you're going to do with it. You might have a vague idea, but you need that abandon to be brilliant at it and to be able to take those risks. That's what I love about Hindustani.

Nirmal: *Who's your favourite singer?*

Kiran: At the moment it's Mukul Shivputra. I adore him. I think he has the most wonderful voice. Rashid Khan is also a great favourite. Among women I've heard Veena Sahasrabuddhe, live, in performance and she's brilliant. Who else do I like—all the old greats, of course. Of them whom I like really is Alladiya Khan. He was one of the few people who weren't limited by *gharana*s. He sang just spectacularly.

Nirmal: *How did Bengali music, Rabindra Sangeet, inspire you?*

Kiran: Rabindra Sangeet was nice. The thing is that we heard a lot of it because of just living in Calcutta. I didn't particularly have some great connection with it, I must say. I feel that in Rabindra Sangeet, the poetry is what the best part of it is. I mean like there are some that we all know such as *Jodi Tor Dak Shune* or *Aalo Aamar Aalo*, which we sang in school. Actually, the poetry in them is quite beautiful. But the melodies and the way of singing for one used to sound quite repetitive, and secondly, I used to find it exceedingly mournful. I like straightforward, good voice sing-your-bit kind of singing.

Nirmal: *There is a snobbishness attached to schools like Loreto and La Martiniere—did it make you like that as well?*

Kiran: I don't think I was ever snobbish, but we were very interested to know what others read, who their favourite authors were; we used to judge people by these things. Like when we went to a school prom, we'd ask the boy what music he listened to, and if he said that he listened to some nonsense type of thing, then we'd just be like 'okay, cancel—next'. That was our way of being snobbish.

But even when I was quite young, I was very keen to strike out on my own. Literally, I wanted to leave home after the 10th standard and go somewhere for my 11th and 12th, but my parents managed to contain me till I was 18. I was keen on Delhi. At that time, I was very interested in development work and I wanted to do Developmental Economics and then maybe later do a business degree. So I wanted to come to Delhi, go to St. Stephens and major in Economics. That was my intention. My parents were dead set against Delhi. They said, *dilli toh nahin bhejenge akele ladki ko*. So it was decided that I could go either to Bombay, Pune or go to Bangalore where they were moving. My father had retired by the time I finished school. So they said, 'come to Bangalore'. I said that I wanted to be alone, be on my own. So I kind of scouted out Pune, but Pune just wasn't for me. Then I finally came to Bombay.

Even in Bombay, I was keen on Xavier's because it was a cool college. I'd been in an all-girls school till I was in class 10. In classes 11 and 12, boys were in a separate school but at least there were some around. And I thought Xavier's would be nice. But my parents said, 'nothing doing, no going to a college which doesn't have a hostel for girls', which struck Xavier's off the list. So the best college with a hostel was Sophia's. It was and is a very good college. The level of instruction and professors were very good. So I got into a hostel, and my sister was married and living in Bombay by then, so my parents were comfortable with me being in Bombay — with someone to keep an eye on me. I've been the least wavered kid but either way my parents wanted someone to report that I was not out painting the town red every day.

So I came to Bombay and did college here. Here in Bombay University, you take three subjects and in the third year, you decide whether you want to do a single major or a double major. You don't really have the Honours system. So what I did take was Economics and Statistics because I thought I wanted to do Economics. But literature has always been my first love. That was the third subject and I loved it. I had some of the best lecturers teaching me literature, poetry and I had the best time. Once I was in the third year, my lecturers really asked me why I was being so bullheaded and suggested I do Literature as my major. At that point, I was quite open to the idea of doing either Literature or Economics as Major, but my parents in those days, in 1995, felt that there's no real future in Literature. You ended up being either a journalist or a teacher. You didn't have too many options. So I did an Economics Major and by the end of the year, I realized that I've always struggled with, I don't know, some kind of a Catholic guilt I must have developed from Loreto days (laughs)... this feeling that I've been inordinately fortunate in my life, always had food on the table, a wonderful family, good school, great life... and what can I do to give back in some way. That was driving my need to do Developmental Economics. It was more something I felt that I ought to do rather than what I really wanted to do. What I really wanted to do was something creative. Because I was always the clown in school — if teachers had a little extra time they would put me on the platform and so I would just tell stories and entertain people — that was my job in school. I was into dramatics, debates and all the creative activities. I wasn't really into sports or studies though I did pretty okay.

So I asked myself why I was fighting this side. I wouldn't have been honest if I had done what I was doing as a sense of duty rather than do what I love. I wasn't sure if film studies was exactly what I wanted to do. The option was, of course, Film and Television Institute of India (FTII) and I was not going to do four years of a course if I was not even sure that I wanted to do films. So I made enquiries and found out that the Jamia Mass Communication Research Centre course was sort of designed to give a primer in many different kinds of communication. That was the one I opted to do. And I went to Jamia.

Nirmal: *So from Calcutta to Bombay, and then to Delhi. How did you like Delhi?*

Kiran: I loved it. I really enjoyed Delhi. I still love Delhi. Of course, in those days life was really quite bad, life for women was not easy and we were very poor students. I mean I was doing a Master's degree and my father who had already retired was supporting me through further college, which was very, very good of them. They were really supportive. My parents have been the most ideal parents one can have. They really let me follow my dream in a very clichéd sense of the word. It was a journey I'd undertaken with no immediate goal in sight. They still said, '*chalo beta, go for it*'. Their point was that so long as you are economically and financially independent, we are happy for you. There was never any pressure to hurry up, finish this and get married.

So I enjoyed Delhi a lot, even though I did struggle with the lack of being able to go anywhere easily; I was very poor. I couldn't really take autos and was mostly travelling by bus. In buses, it was fair game—people pinching. But the initial days in Delhi, I had a very soft landing because I stayed in New Friends Colony, which is next door to Jamia. So I could literally walk or take the cycle rickshaw. Thereafter, I moved to Mayur Vihar because I thought it'd be cheaper, though it wasn't cheaper as I was always taking autos. There was one bus from Mayur Vihar that started just two stops before my house but there were people on the roof and there was no way to get on to it (laughs). After that I moved to Sukhdev Vihar, which was much closer. But I loved the Delhi experience.

College was great; I made some of my best friends there. When I think about it now, I think the course was very well designed. Essentially, they gave you a little bit of a peak into everything. They had courses such as Visual Communication, which Rajeev Lochan—now Head of the National Gallery of Modern Art—had designed. It was in the first year, so it was a whole year and really luxurious. The course was very unusual. He made you take bits of something like chart paper, and he was kind of getting you used to the fact that you are going to essentially create dimension and depth on a two-dimensional surface-like film. So how does one actually give the impression of texture, depth and light on a two-dimensional surface? So with that paper he would give you a project to give depth… it was quite complicated but very interesting. Every week we would discuss our work and he had a very freewheeling discussion, like we would go through food, music, just anything, talk about anything. I think the course left a lot of room for general ideas and discussion. I enjoyed the course a lot. Of course, to be honest, we had poor photography, cameras… the visual side of the course was not so good.

Preeti: *Did they also offer some internship — as in hands-on training on any particular project?*

Kiran: No, no. We had to make our own short film. My budgets were cut and we got less than the previous year but you had to make your own short film — continuity exercise, sync sound exercise, and then we made our final films. Right through that period, I was thinking that maybe I wanted to be a cinematographer because I was really interested in visuals. That was what got me going. In the first two projects you had to do everything—you had to shoot, edit, do the sound, pretty much do everything. For the final project, only eight films were made. There would be three people in each team—a director, an editor and a sound designer, and one camera person. So we had to give our preferences, as you know, whether you want to do editing or something else. My preference was to do cinematography. But also, each and every person had to handle a script. So they would choose eight scripts that they liked and those eight people would get to be directors. My script was chosen and I was asked why I wanted to do cinematography. To which I said that I liked telling the story through pictures. They said, 'If you want to tell a story then show someone else how you want the pictures to be'. What they meant to ask was whether I wanted to capture pictures for somebody else's story or tell my own story. They explained to me in a different way what a director did. Then I actually realized that I wanted to create that picture and creating that picture is the director's job. What that is picture about and why it is there in the first place—that is a director's job.

Preeti: *A lot of the other film directors who we have interviewed do not have any formal training in filmmaking. How difficult is the transition into filmmaking? Also, did your coming from a film school hamper your growth as a film director or did it add to it?*

Kiran: That's a very interesting question. If you ask me today, I would always say that some amount of technical or artistic training is very important before you set out on a job. But I have to say that when I left film school I thought that I'd be able to make a film within two years. I left in 1998 and said that in 2000, I will make a film. It took me five years to even be able to write a script. So I don't think film school prepares you necessarily to be able to make a film. I think what it does is make you, in a holistic way, a more artistic person—if it's a good film school. It gives the artistic tools and gives you aesthetic judgment, which you may or may not get if you're working in the field because you'll be surrounded by people who are doing mediocre work or even if you're used to training yourself and are a very diligent person, and train yourself outside of work by watching very good cinema or immersing yourself in good literature and good music.... I mean it is a luxury to be just entirely immersed in study of an artistic kind, is something that informs you in a very deep way. But when you come out you realize that you have to know the world that you're working in and so it's very important to work in the field as well. People who've worked in the field have already had those physical and networking skills set to make a film. Now do they have an aesthetic? If they are good, creative, really bright minds, then they might. But I think a combination of both is required. That's what I got and therefore it took me much longer because I did not just spend two or two-and-a-half years studying film but also three or four years entirely only working with film directors in different kinds of films.

Nirmal: *When you are part of a film school and you've seen the best of world cinema, isn't there a pulling towards that kind of aesthetic? Most of the people I've spoken to say that this aesthetic becomes somewhat of an impediment in their filmmaking because though they are influenced by world cinema, at the end of the day, they have to make middle-class, Bollywood-inspired films.*

Kiran: I know what you mean, but it depends on what kind of film you're committed to make. When I came out of Jamia, within a year or two people were telling me that I should make ad-films as I would make double the money I was making as an AD. What double, you'll make hundred times the money you're making as an AD. But I was so much a purist that I couldn't imagine creating images for this kind of monetary set up where you have to show a chocolate for one and a half second and you have to cast a particular kind of woman. It just wasn't palatable to me though it would have been extremely easy for me; thereafter, I had done commercials to jump out and make a film. But I think it's an impediment if you want to be making the kind of films that everybody is making. I have never been interested in just making films because I have to churn out work—maybe this has been in some ways an impediment but has nothing to do with me being in film school. My point has been that if something deeply interests me, the process of which is highly inspiring, then I'll make a film.... Making films for me was never because I wanted a career in films. It's really odd, but I'm extremely happy making my living either as an AD or a producer, but I feel, as a director if I have to do something it should be really what I want to do... it's a very personal thing for me.

Nirmal: *Having gone to a film school, were you inspired to make a certain kind of cinema?*

Kiran: I think it was much later that I saw films that I wanted to emulate. *Memories of Underdevelopment* by a Tomás Gutiérrez Alea—I remember seeing this film and being overwhelmed! Another film was *Hiroshima Mon Amour* and for some reason Robert Bresson's movies.... I enjoyed his films a lot though they were very austere and strange kind of films. I liked the usual Buñuel and everyone else. I loved *Nights of Cabiria*—Federico Fellini always managed to do that, give you a superb plot and lots of drama and still remain 'non-plotty' in the way that we know it. The internal drama was something that excited him so much. I loved all these filmmakers. For me, the world of images, writing, music, photography, textures, space and history—all of these—come together in this beautiful medium. So for me, it is important to find that story that can use all these well and that also in some way drives me closer to understanding what makes us who we are and what makes people tick. That is the kind of film I'd always wanted to make. So it's always been a very personal journey. It had to be something that I felt answered some of the most basic questions of why we are around. People, their motives, interest me—just general characters, just images of people, how they live their lives interests me the most. Genuinely, I only want to make films that help me know myself a little bit. So as I write, it has to illuminate something for me, otherwise I don't want to write at all.

Nirmal: *Autobiographical?*

Kiran: Not autobiographical, but something that helps me understand human nature—the human condition.

Nirmal: *Was Shai you? Both Shai and the girl in the videotape are you. Also, the guys are known actors but the girl is unknown.*

Kiran: Actually, all three of them in my opinion were unknown. I was looking, in fact, for all four unknown. *Prateek ko koi nahin jaanta tha aur Kriti Malhotra to costume assistant thi.* And Monica was a singer. I wanted everyone unknown. Aamir came in and changed the mix a bit, and even Prateek was fairly unknown. It was a conscious decision.

Nirmal: *No, what I mean is that how much of a film is autobiographical, any film?*

Kiran: Well, I suppose if you write your own work there are definitely impressions, whole incidents or whole characters that you somehow weave into your film, consciously or unconsciously. In some way, it'll have your point of view on life.

I haven't been consciously autobiographical in *Dhobi Ghat*. I know that a lot of the things that the film deals with are things that I'm personally obsessed with. Such as the old part of the city of Bombay.

Preeti: *It is interesting that though a large part of your life was spent in Calcutta and that's where your roots are, you chose Bombay as the setting of your first movie....*

Kiran: Strangely, that's not the case. I think I know Bombay much better. Of course, now my years in Bombay equal those in Calcutta, but you see when you come to a new place, you explore much more whereas in Calcutta I lived in my little world. I don't actually know that much about the hinterland—we didn't travel in Bengal that much. So, to be honest, Bombay was home. When I came here, I felt a certain kind of freedom as a young adult, an exciting life as a single person, not knowing anybody, not knowing the place. I used to live in a hostel; so the little time I would get away from college, I would take a bus and go to South Bombay, spend time in the old second-hand bookshops. I remember South Bombay on Saturdays or Sundays, a lovely bus ride along Marine Drive, going to Fort where the second-hand bookshops were, and eating guavas and peanuts—that's my memory of Bombay. When I arrived in Bombay, it was literally one of those clichéd things, when you get off the train and feel—Now I've come home. I had that feeling when I came to Bombay. That's why I'll always be obsessed with the city.

When I was in the hostel, I used to travel so much by bus and train. My sister was in Chembur, I had my orthodontist in Bandra, all the art galleries and everything else was in South Bombay—so I travelled a lot around Bombay, so much so that I know Bombay much better than most people who've lived there all their lives. I enjoy these little gullies, little shops and old buildings. I used to walk down them, on my own, on many afternoons and explore for the fun of it. That for me has always been the city of Bombay. It's not only the high rises, big cars and people—it's always been old streets, quaint old shops and trains. The interesting thing about Bombay is how you see it—actually it is a construct of our imagination in many ways. For me, it is the lovely rounded *chawl* old buildings with the tiled roofs, which is in the old parts of the city—Mohammad Ali Road, Dadar, the Parsi Colony.

Nirmal: You stayed there in a house for 15-20 days during shooting Dhobi Ghat.

Kiran: Yes, we lived in that house because it was such a small *gully* that a car literally goes at less than walking pace round the gully. So if Aamir had travelled by car, it would have created a riot there. It was his idea. That was one big reason that I didn't want to cast him in the film because I said that I wanted to shoot in real locations, I wanted the character to walk down Khau gully during Ramzan and that was two million people at any given point of time.

Nirmal: Let's go back a little. You joined the film industry as a third AD in Lagaan. *That was when you came to a 'real' set. How was that experience?*

Kiran: The set was wonderful. For one-and-a-half years I had been in advertising. When I came to a film set I expected it to be so different. I expected it to be very unprofessional.

That was the impression of film productions—*script nahin hota hai*. But this was the complete opposite. It was the first big commercial film to do work in this first AD system, which had now become a norm for big films. It was the first big film to do live sound—sync sound. So these were huge production nightmares for any production to handle because you're doing it in one schedule, you're doing sync sound, you have an AD system that requires you have a bound script and have a very detailed idea of what you're doing everyday. Needless to say, it was an extremely professional set up. *Lagaan* was maybe one of the first Hindi films that made Hindi films professional. It became a standard. Everybody thereafter, whether it was Excel Films or Vinod Chopra Productions, or Yash Raj, started doing all their films in sync sound. Before that, small films were doing it, especially when there was foreign funding: *Earth* did live sound, then *Fire*, but not a big film.

I think *Lagaan* also made it easier for women to be part of filmmaking because it was a professional set up—not like *haan ji, haan ji*, where the AD is holding a *Pan Parag dabba*. We had delineated, fixed jobs and my job was to take care of actors through hair, make-up and wardrobe. It was a nightmare because there were 82 people if you look at the cast list, and at any given point of time there were 11 members of one team, 11 of the other. So there were 30 or 35 people to get ready. I was the first person to reach the set and the last person to leave it. It was physically very very tough.

Nirmal: *When you joined the film, Ashutosh Gowariker was not a well-known director. Aamir was the only star, really. What was your first impression of the film?*

Kiran: To be honest, when I read the script, I said, '*haan theek hai*'. I had no notion of films. You have to remember that I must have seen, in my conscious memory, less than 10

Hindi films. So I had no real context within which to view this script. I had seen only good films. I had seen *Sholay, Qayamat Se Qayamat Tak, Dilwale Dulhania Le Jayenge* — films that were big hits. So when I read the script it wasn't like I said 'What an unusual script' because I did not know what the norm was. I wasn't steeped in that filmi culture. I was used to advertising so when I came here and as it was a professional set up, I thought it was great as we were on the same level. So I didn't find anything unusual. Even if there were well-known actresses I may not have known them. I mean I would have known 'Madhuri' but not watched all her films. Aamir was one of the few people I knew — I had already seen three of his films, which were *Qayamat Se Qayamat Tak, Jo Jeeta Wohi Sikander* and *Rangeela*. I had not seen any of his other films. My first impression was that I could do this. I wasn't introduced to the filmmaking of the previous decade where there was no script. It was like *writer aaya hai set par, us din ke scenes likh raha hai*. It's a morning shot and the actor has not come. That was how films were made, and maybe still are. I came to a set where four in the morning meant Aamir in the bus at four in the morning. Everybody travelled by bus. There is no private car. *Lagaan* is sort of a textbook film; I mean you'll never get a film like *Lagaan*. It was the single most, unique film for the way in which it was made — and that contributed to its massive reception.

Nirmal: *Did you have an idea that the movie would be a blockbuster?*

Kiran: No. But we all were called to see an early cut, which was four hours without the climax. They just called a bunch of us to see it and give a reaction and I thought it was superb fun. I just loved it. When we were shooting it, I was like, *yaar yeh gaane, kya hai*. I was totally from the world of no song and dance in films. But when I saw it, totally swept away by it. At that time I remember coming out and telling Aamir, Reena, Raosahib and all the production team that I thought it would be a super hit. Well, it was. I think it was the single most important thing to happen to a lot of us who worked on it. It changed the way we approached our own work. It raised the bar for all of us. We couldn't go back to doing some nonsense.

Nirmal: *You were a third AD on the sets of* Lagaan. *What was your take on your own job?*

Kiran: What I was doing was incredibly uncreative, which was the dreariest part of it. Ultimately, in filmmaking when you come down to a set, it's creative only for the actor and the director. Other people are cogs in the wheel. *Aapko light idhar ghoomana hai, udhar ghoomana hai; aapko actor tayyar karna hai, aapko trolley push karna hai*—it was physical work for six months in the heat of Kutch. After a point, it became very frustrating, and it was getting very tiring but it was one of those few films where they gave one day off in a week, which films don't do normally. It was a very well run set, but it could get fatiguing—six months doing the same job. So on more than one occasion I thought I should quit. I have learnt what I had to learn, and I should go. But I remember Anil Mehta, the director of photography (DP), telling me that I'd stuck it out for four months and should see it to the end—that I would be happy. I was so happy he talked me out of quitting because it was one of the best things I ever did in my life.

What I used to do was to get the actors ready and then I had to—what they call—'lock up' in the make-up room, which means ensuring that nobody makes a sound during the take. When you hear 'lock up' you make sure everybody knows around you that the take has started. Then you have to make sure nobody makes a sound until 'cut'. After 'cut' everybody goes back to talking. That was my job. Three-fourth of the time all the actors were on set. *So kissi ko lock up bhi nahin karna tha, do ya chaar log the jo so rahe hote the.* So I have read so many books sitting there. With my head in a book suddenly I'd say 'lock it up' then I'd hear 'cut' and back to my book. But it was a great time. We were such a big family, we shared an apartment, we used to cook, we used to make clothes, *arrey kitne tailor ke visits the hamare* — we really enjoyed Bhuj. Bhuj was one of the nicest towns I had ever shot in before the whole thing fell down. There was the Old Market road. Of course after the earthquake it all crumbled... but really we had the best time. We used to have party after party every weekend. *Dry state mein hum log ne pata nahi kitni daaru pee thi.*

Preeti: *What were the projects that you did professionally post-*Lagaan?

Kiran: I came back to Bombay and I desperately needed to earn money so I went back to advertising.

Preeti: *Were you financially stable by then?*

Kiran: Advertising was fairly well paying and in *Lagaan*, it was average. I would not say it was superb but they were paying adequately. I was the third AD. So I earned what I would for my first film. Now when you look at what ADs are paid, they are paid a hell of a lot in feature films. You'd be surprised that the impression of the film industry is that it's very exploitative, but if you go and see the lowest paid worker in the film industry earns thousand rupees a day. That is the spot boy. So the film industry is a very well paying job to have unless you're a trainee or a fresh AD — then you might get paid like ₹10,000 a month. More often than not ₹10,000 is the starting salary in the film industry, which is a good salary by any standards. You get paid usually by the week so it's even better. After *Lagaan*

I came back and did advertising for a couple of years—I used to freelance. I did a lot of work with Highlight and with Corcoise, which is Prasoon Pandey's company. I was the first AD there—that was my role. Generally, you only come in for the shoot, do your job and go. Maybe a day of pre-production, but generally you run a set.

Preeti: *Was being a freelancer a little tough? Did you have any professional insecurity?*

Kiran: To be honest it was not tough. I think I was paid so well. In fact, I lived a great life. Even in those days my salary was decent enough for me to afford an apartment on my own. In 1999, 13 years ago, I was paying ₹12,000 rent, which meant it was half my salary, but in Bombay, it's normal. Of course, I spent all my money because living here is also expensive. But I lived well. After I finished *Lagaan*, I lived in Bandra and before that I used to live in South Bombay—till 2000. I rented different places—I've lived in so many different apartments, I've lost count. Lived well enough to have a computer, upgrade it ever so often and buy a car. I was well off. I had no savings, but I would go on holidays, go out to eat and drink.

Preeti: *Are you an outdoor person? Do you travel a lot?*

Kiran: I used to be a very outdoor person. I used to enjoy Delhi for that reason. The main reason I loved Delhi was its proximity to the hills. If I got three days off, my friends and I would jazz off to Narkanda, Dalhousie. I like the outdoors—I like mountains the most. I love cities. I love to travel. Unfortunately, I don't get to do that anymore. I only travel to locations that one shoots in. I like nature a lot and I like cities a lot because of culture. I'm not into adventure sports, but you give me a bird park or a beach or mountains and I am set. I love to swim as well.

Brave New Bollywood

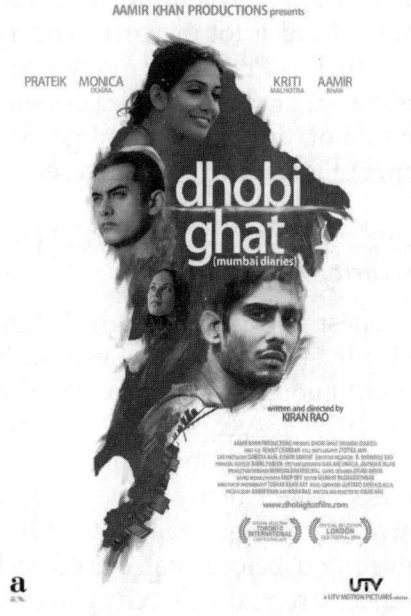

Courtesy: Kiran Rao.

Preeti: *So when did you start writing* Dhobi Ghat?

Kiran: I started writing it in early 2005. Aamir was shooting for *Rang de Basanti*. I thought it was a great opportunity to go on a writing holiday because they were shooting in Delhi, Punjab….

Preeti: *What was your equation with Aamir, by then?*

Kiran: We were living together. We had been living together since June, 2004. We got married in December, 2005.

So in the beginning of 2005, when he went off to shoot *Rang De Basanti* in Ludhiana and Amritsar, I thought it would be a good way for me to focus on my writing. Even though I had stopped doing AD work to write, it was 2004 and I wasn't able to get anything done. I had written one test screenplay and I kept calling it test because I didn't know whether I could write. I had never written anything until then. So I wrote a story, not a screenplay but a script kind of outline, in 2004 and it wasn't bad. I thought that now I had practice because the fact was to get over the fear and inhibitions in your mind when you were writing for the first time. I felt this would be a good trip to make; I'll go with Aamir and use this time to write. It was the best thing I've ever done. I'm a very social person, I enjoy meeting people and I enjoy going out, eating, travelling because of which my energies would get dispersed very easily. People would call me and want to hang out. So when they were shooting *Rang De Basanti*, they would all leave the hotel at 6 or 6:30 in the morning. I would get up at 6:30, and I had a whole day of writing till they came back at 6 in the evening. Nobody knew me in Ludhiana and Amritsar. Nobody to ring the doorbell, *ki bhai dhobi aaya hai*. I would just order breakfast, lunch and then by evening they'd all come and then we'd all hang out and have fun. So it was literally like a writing trip and that's when I actually got a chunk of my writing done.

Nirmal: *Were you a trained scriptwriter?*

Kiran: No, not at all. In fact that's one thing they don't teach at Jamia. They don't teach you to write at all. Even in cinematography, we learned the basics of everything, but the next day if they'd given me some other camera I wouldn't have known exactly what to do. Cinematography is one part of your course.

Nirmal: *You had an idea about the script?*

Kiran: You discover the story as you write it. In my kind of story there's not a plot that's *ki dekho ek ladki hai*, she's married to somebody, she kills her husband, she's on the run and in the end she meets this guy and she's saved by him. *Aisa koi plot hota* then you can tell a screenwriter that I want this, it's set in Meerut, *ladki* is from this background and *ladka* is from that. But in mine there was no plot. So it was in the writing that I developed and explored those characters — as I wrote them. That I think is actually the best way to write a screenplay.

I'd been discussing it with a lot of writers later and they said, 'Nowadays even in American film schools, they ask you not to write a character sketch'. You're limiting your character that way. You start off with an idea — there's a guy who wants to be a pilot. As you're writing it, you discover that this guy is very jealous of this other person or he has a deep love for his mother. If you set these limits as you start, then you're already boxing your character and making sure that when a situation arises you've already determined his reaction to it. Whereas, if you've left that open, then you can really play around with the character. You're sending a character out into this world, and then when you put up a situation, then in his reactions to that situation, you realize Oh! he's also very possessive or Oh! he's this or Oh! he's that. That process of discovery is the most exciting part about writing.

To my mind, filmmaking is not about being on the set. It's about honing your writing skills, discovering characters, discovering places as you write. Even then it becomes very difficult because it's a very lonely experience and very challenging too. That's the best thing about writing a screenplay — I would love it if somebody would give me a screenplay, which is the way I see things, the way I look at characters. For instance, I really enjoy the writings of Anjum Hasan. She has written three novels and one collection of stories. I feel that might be the kind of mind that fits my idea of a screenplay. Otherwise I don't know anybody whose work I can directly read and say, 'I want to make this into a film'. In the process of writing, I discover why I'm writing it. I don't set out with the idea that I want to tell a story about revenge. It's more like a journey of discovery and exploration. When I write, I explore motives; I explore reasons as to why the story interests me. So it could easily be a failure because you might reach that road and see that actually this story doesn't interest me in a deeper way. It's only when you start writing it that you realize it *ki bhai is character mein koi dam nahin hai.*

Preeti: *In the case of* Dhobi Ghat, *did you have some idea or did it evolve as you wrote it?*

Kiran: I had some ideas. I had two situations that were interesting for me. One was this relationship between the dhobi and the client, and not just the role of class but also identity, how we see ourselves, and how they relate to each other outside of these class boundaries, and what would happen if there were an attraction or love in that equation? Is it possible for anything to happen? Those questions interested me. So that was one.

The other was the idea of these clips that somebody finds, a kind of diary of this woman who is from a very different background but, in a sense, completely connects emotionally with this person and changes the way he looks at life, looks at the city.

That journey is the most interesting thing about writing. For instance, this script that I'm trying to write on Gauhar Jaan, I already had a character that you know certain public facts about, and I'm just finding it very difficult to write because there's history there, so I have to be accurate.

Nirmal: *When we're watching the film, we realize that Arun was not written in the beginning — he's a recluse and you've hardly* *given the poor guy any dialogue, I mean, there are no punches. Aamir's a superstar, which doesn't come across in this film. Was it difficult for you to induct him later?*

Kiran: I have known him personally for so long. In a sense, he's a very private person. He's not a very party-going, outdoor person.... Well, he likes going to parties on occasion, but he's not a party person. When I was writing the script, I wanted somebody who didn't say very much but who had very expressive eyes and was able to communicate with a certain intensity and depth without having to say much — through body language, his eyes and minimal expression. I used to think of him often for that. That's the reason I didn't find it hard to put him in that role.

Nirmal: Somehow I felt very strongly that Aamir would have been very good in the dhobi's role.

Kiran: If he had been younger he would have been perfect. I don't know if it's there in the DVD but we have all the screen tests in the Blu-ray — of each of them there's one. But Aamir used to keep saying that *yaar mujhe Munna ka role karna hai*. In the script, I had specified Munna's age. I wanted him to be younger than the girl. And I was quite sure that I wanted the artist to be a middle aged, in his thirties, sort of person who's seen enough of life to be jaded by these art openings and this fake art scene.

Nirmal: Did Aamir learn how to paint for the film?

Kiran: Artists came to the set and had to teach him how to paint. In fact, I spent a lot of time with Ravi who did the paintings. I spent a lot of time in his studio because you imagine that they sit, and look, and paint... but Ravi uses a sponge, or a scalpel, or throws things and wipes things off. His work is abstract but it's very revealing... with different layers... through accretion and reduction. It was an interesting thing for all of us to learn. Ravi would come to the set and do the shot and we used to work with acrylics... so we literally used to wipe it off and Aamir would just copy him. It was fun. The best experience that I've ever had in my life was while shooting *Dhobi Ghat*.

Nirmal: *The film shows that you were immensely in love with him (Aamir Khan). Of course you're looking through the camera... the physicality of the scene is very obvious like sometimes when the sun is falling on him.... It is one of the best shots of Aamir I have seen. If I am in love with someone and I make a film with them, it will show.*

Kiran: I am sure it does. I was deeply in love with him and I still am.

Nirmal: *All films are voyeuristic, but this film is voyeuristic at multiple levels. One, there is a videotape that Arun watches. Another is Aamir being looked at by Shai. The third is that as a director you are looking at Munna. Multiple voyeurisms come from your film school training – was it a conscious effort on your part?*

Kiran: Yes. You know what I was talking about the city being a construct. I hate to sound academic, but I feel that our various ways of viewing the city make the city real in that way. For instance, you are a person who lives in Koliwada, a fisherman by trade, and what you see of the city is the city for you. My view of the city is the city. If you take me to the Koli village today, I will say, 'This is not Bombay for me, this is a village'. This is pretty much what I wanted to say about the city – all these ways of seeing are what make this city and account for the multiplicity of experiences in the city. I didn't want to have it as just my way of seeing through my script. I wanted to represent each character's way of seeing in some way.

In this case, how does a small-town Muslim girl view a city the first time she's seeing the ocean, these big buildings and this fast-paced life—what is her experience of the city? And so you have her diaries. Then, how Aamir's character relates to the city is through his work, you see it through his paintings. So his first show is called 'Buildings', which is really about people who build the city and never get a place to live in it themselves. He's using the city as a muse, which he represents through his paintings. For Shai, she's really the ultimate tourist—she intrudes. She's the person for whom the city is, in a sense, the exotic. Her black and white lens is capturing people who do regular, menial jobs, but she's doing portraiture of the common man. Whereas portraiture is normally the privy of kings, queens—rich people. She's giving the common person the space of a portrait. So how we have seen the city is to create these beautiful black and white portraits of a fish seller or a knife sharpener. And they have this dignity looking into the camera and you see their lives through her eyes, the eyes of a privileged person who has the power of the camera, the power of the gaze.

To my mind, all these various ways of seeing were creating levels and layers of the city itself. So the voyeurism was doing that—creating layers of the city, which I would never have been able to create for you if I made it a single narrative. The story has to become about the levels of life in this city where all the intersections of all the sets are shown—that's our city, it's an intersection of millions of sets. Can you imagine how rich it is? It's an intersection of different kinds of people from all over the country. It's traditionally been a harbour, where people have come over centuries to make a livelihood, to trade; convicts have come and people have come over generations to this city. That interests me a lot about Bombay. I think the voyeurism was a way for me to actually look into four stories in this city of millions. I created it also because I wanted it to be visually and texturally rich and diverse. So it's not just one story happening. Each story is texturally and in a narrative way, rich. So the voyeurism was a technique, a fairly academic technique — but visually and in a narrative way. I wanted to do it in a way where it wasn't just a gimmick and wasn't mere technique. It was very much a part of the storytelling device. I was telling the story through these lenses.

Nirmal: *Shai is a photographer and there are a lot of stills. I wanted to talk of the use of stills — a stationary moment — in the movie. You have some kind of artistic interest in moments.*

Kiran: I feel photography is to film like what poetry is to literature. It will tell you in just one frame, a distilled moment, what a whole film will tell, sometimes. To my mind, the power of that is something I had to have in my film. Sometimes, just one person looking into the camera, you'll see a whole life in front of you, which you'll never be able to otherwise.

Preeti: *Your film is doing what a lot of other films are also trying to do — showing how sex is delinked from any false morality and social institutions — particularly marriage. I was intrigued though, when the otherwise liberal Shai gets upset with Arun after their one night stand and walks out of the house.*

Kiran: Because for one, I think, she thought there was something special there and that he was cool enough to not go down the road of 'Oh! She expects this from me' and actually acknowledge that they had a good time and that they had shared something, which most men are paranoid about. She would have thought that he gets up in the morning, they are cool, they have breakfast and they say they'll call each other, if and when they want — a friendship begins there. But he is of a completely different headspace and he's gone through bad relationships. He's an island unto himself. He doesn't want to open himself up to anyone. So he gets almost paranoid that there's a woman in his house, in his personal space. So the kind of vibe he gives her is one of rejection and that it is insulting.

Nirmal: *But you change the character because later Arun doesn't think of her that much but Shai still can't forget him. While she gets out of his life she can't get him out of her mind and she keeps searching and asking, and finally, you show Munna giving her the address. Finally, you have Indianized it.*

Kiran: This is not Indianizing—this is character. She thought there was something very special and that night was a very special night for her. She was interested in the guy. Now see, I didn't marry Aamir within a day. I lived with him for one-and-a-half years before we decided to get married. So I come from a similar background where if I get intimate with someone one day I'm not expecting him to marry me. I would like us to go out, maybe for six months just go dating, we'll meet on occasion, assess each other, have fun together—that's what any modern, urban woman would do. So she's from that background. But you see, she actually did quite fancy him; she was interested in him. Actually, in many ways, when something is not available to you, you're much more obsessed with it. So today, if you tell me that you don't want to have a relationship with me, then I can't get you out of my mind. But if I've spent more than three days with you, I'll say, '*Yaar, yeh aadmi thoda ajeeb hai*'. But within one hour, if we have a superb conversation, after which you say that let's not be in touch, then I won't be able to get you out of my mind. There's that possibility of something great with you that has not been explored. So that plays on her mind. Also, thoughts like 'did that night mean nothing?' or 'was I so uninteresting?' *Usne darwaza* *bandh karke mujhe bhaga diya*. We danced, we talked, and it was a magical night, when you connect with somebody. It wasn't about the sex; that memory of her's you see, there is very little that is sexual, it's more to do with intimacy. They are talking about pictures, they are dancing, and they are talking and laughing. Those are things that we all, most romantics, feel is the epitome of romance when you actually connect with someone in a deep way. Like, we talked about all the things I love or that he has such an interesting perspective on so many things. *Yeh mera take tha on Shai*. So she can't get him out of her mind because of that. She thinks that they would have been great together, not to marry, but just to be with because they got on so well.

Nirmal: *Finance wouldn't have been a problem for this film.*

Kiran: Finance would have been a problem had Aamir not liked it. But I was very lucky—Aamir really loved the script. Even when I was unsure about it, he saw the potential in it. He told me, of course, what he found problematic. What you see is 99% what my first screenplay draft was—it was a good first draft. I wasn't expecting Aamir to produce it. He was paranoid actually. He said, '*Kuch likhegi*, I'll say it's bad and she'll be very upset'. Luckily, it worked out. But creatively, I was very sure that I'd only make this film the way I wanted to make it, which was a very independent kind of way—with a very small team, very real locations, hopefully, untrained actors—new actors. I produced it myself in the sense that I created a sort of small production company while I was going looking for locations because I knew that the second Aamir Khan Production's name came in, it would be impossible to shoot without paying a huge amount of money. I created a small company so that I could shoot like an independent filmmaker.... It was still very expensive because shooting in Bombay is expensive, regardless. But right through the production time, I produced it entirely myself. Aamir Khan Production's muscle came in only after I had finished shooting. Aamir, of course, came in and helped me immensely in my edit, because the pace of this film is a very difficult one to strike, and so we took a long time to edit it. Then Aamir gave me the music director of my choice, distribution, and all of that Aamir Khan Production took care of. But creatively, I was lucky to have independence.

Preeti: *There are some scenes which I felt were very important. Like the second time when Arun bumps into Shai and invites her for coffee to his place. While she's there, Munna arrives to deliver the clothes and the way her expression changes. And it is heartwarming when she follows him trying to placate him* 'haan, coffee ke liye jayenge, film ke liye jayenge'.

Another one is where Munna comes to her house to deliver clothes and the maid offers him tea in an old rejected glass and Shai promptly takes it from him and hands him her own cup. That was such a poignant scene.

Kiran: Absolutely. I mean, today, to eat a meal say sitting with your maid is unthinkable. My driver won't sit on the same table; I still take him to the restaurants that I eat in but *woh always alag table par baith kar khata hai. Usko bhi acha lagta hai,* that's what I feel. *Kyunki agar mere saath baithta toh* he would have to have a conversation with me but anywhere else in the world you go on a production run, the driver sits with you, you all sit on the same table and everybody eats. This is Third-World, Southeast Asia specific — the help doesn't have the same space.

Nirmal: *Has the world become easier being Mrs Aamir Khan — as a director?*

Kiran: Interesting. I would say that I've had maybe more film experiences of the world because I'm Mrs Aamir Khan. I've been for more festivals, I've travelled a lot with Aamir, met a lot of huge head honchos of every possible studio.

Nirmal: If you do a film there will be 20 people lined up to support you.

Kiran: You know people are not so foolish anymore. I'm a big name. If I can bring Aamir in my film everybody will line up, but today, the kind of film I'm making I don't think everybody will line up to produce or release my film. So people don't necessarily give you money because you're a big name. That, I have to tell you, in life is a fact. I find that it's probably easier if you've done 20 housefuls before you try and get money for the next film. But definitely life is easier because doors open. I'm able to have access to so many things, to even dream of getting Gustavo to do the music on my film — if it was being produced by somebody else, *unke paas na interest hota na paisa*. Aamir asked me — who do you want, if you had anybody in the world, who would it be? I said, Gustavo. He said, *'chalo, dekhte hain, woh free hai, usko karna hai ki nahin'*. No producer does that. Not even the best producers do that. Definitely, life has become easier on a film level.

Preeti: When it comes to contemporary filmmakers, who is your favourite?

Kiran: My favourite is Dibakar. He's far ahead of anyone else. I greatly enjoy his work and I'm quite envious of it. I love his films. I like his head, his eye. Other than him I would say the other person whose films I enjoy and would go to see would be Anurag. Who else? I like Raju Hirani.

I enjoyed whatever films I've seen of his. I also enjoyed Imtiaz Ali's *Jab We Met*.

Preeti: *And Aamir?*

Kiran: And Aamir as a director, of course. I would go to watch anything that Imtiaz made. Vishal—I like his sensibility.

Preeti: *Do you think what we call the multiplex cinema will last? My take is it's not going to last much. Big films have already taken over and there's no space for small films.*

Kiran: Yes, and I feel the reason for that is very complicated and it'll take me a long time to explain. But I agree with you. The fact is that what the multiplex was supposed to do was give you an option to be able to show a film in a small theatre—with just about 100 or 200 people. *Woh khatam kisliye ho raha hai ki aap single screen mein, maaniye aapka rent 5,000 tak hai din ka,* even if nobody wants to release my film and it's a small film, I'll take the risk myself. Whereas, in a multiplex they decide whether they want to give it to you or not, and second, they never give it to you as rental, they only do sharing with you. They can throw out the film at any time. So your film has to be a blockbuster to be able to survive.

So take a film like, say, *Shanghai*, which supposedly is a big film, but it's a niche film in many ways, or take *LSD: Love, Sex Aur Dhokha*, which should run because it's a good film. And it is very likely that after the first week, it will pick up. *But ek week ke andar multiplex dekhti hai ki arrey 20 log baithe hain, nikalo film ko.* So it'll get thrown out. Whereas in a rental theatre, I can still say that I will pay the rent, *abhi logon ko achi lag rahi hai,* I can take that risk. Unfortunately, small filmmakers don't have that option. The multiplex throws you out if you're not a hit. So unless you deliver a hit... a film like *Dhobi Ghat* isn't an instant hit, a formula film or a film like *Udaan* — it is not a film that will necessarily draw huge audiences for weeks and weeks together. They'll have a smaller audience; you'll need a small theatre, a 200 seater.

Nirmal: *A film like* Antardwand *was pulled down before I could reach it. It was there for just one day.*

Kiran: You see what is important for us is to create alternative screening options for non-mainstream or niche films. I'm very keen on doing it. American multiplex doesn't mean that five Hollywood films and three European films are playing. *Aisa nahin hai.* Even in America, there will be eight Hollywood films and Angelika, IFC, Curzon Soho, which show your art house films. So there is a certain kind of venue where you go to see that cinema. That doesn't exist here. This is one of the things that I've already started working on and am interested in doing. I'm actually working on creating an art house cinema space in Bombay.

Nirmal: *Do something in Delhi. Also, there is an elitist assumption that somebody living in the slum will not enjoy a Satyajit Ray film. I used to take cinema to remote areas in the country, such as Bihar or to Sangam Vihar, a big slum area in Delhi. We would tell them* ki yeh Pather Panchali hai, bahut badi film hai, iski yeh storyline hai, isko dekho. *They used to love it. If in my college I show this film, students leave the screening after some time.*

Kiran: Yes, slowly we'll do it all over the country. This is a big struggle. Aamir believes that if it's a good film it translates, but my feeling is that there are certain kinds of cinematic language that you can't easily slip into. For instance, my film, if for people who are not accustomed to watching different kinds of cinema — it is alien — the filmmaking language is alien. *Kahaani kya hai, kya ho raha hai, samajh mein nahin aata*. So, for instance, when I showed it to my staff, such as the drivers, office boys, many of them didn't understand it because there are multiple stories. So it definitely needs a different approach, in distribution, in exhibition, in promotion. We need something different from a mainstream film and you can't be expected to compete with a *Dabangg*. You are competing for theatrical space.

Reema Kagti

Source: Authors.

Filmmaker and screenwriter Reema Kagti was born in Digboi, Assam, to a chemical-engineer father and a teacher mother. She was raised in a typically middle-class household with two other sisters, splitting her childhood years between her parents' plantation farm in the small town of Borhapjan (after her father had hung his spurs at the refinery) and boarding school at Loreto Convent, Shillong. A film fanatic from the beginning, young Reema would frequent the town's club for the weekend movie shows, but that never being enough, she also came to depend on pirated copies, since that was the only other route to Hindi cinema. From the hills, she moved to Delhi Public School (DPS) in Delhi and then finally completed her junior college in Mumbai.

It was Mira Nair's *Salaam Bombay* (1988) that Kagti discovered on an otherwise routine bunking-from-school adventure in Delhi, and it opened her eyes like no other movie had. Defiant as ever, and determined to escape the rigour of the final two school years in Delhi, she shifted to Mumbai to be a part of the gambolling that junior college tolerated, even though her parents wanted her to carry on in Delhi. In retrospect, Kagti feels that the allure of the silver screen was a latent force that guided her actions. Reema then completed her Bachelor's degree in English Literature, followed by a Postgraduate Diploma in Social Communications Media at the Sophia Polytechnic.

This fireball soon landed a job as an AD in Rajat Kapoor's *Private Detective: Two Plus Two One* (1997), which, though unreleased, acquainted her with the basics of script writing, editing and sound. Kagti went on to assist an impressive batch of films, including Kaizad Ustad's *Bombay Boys*, Ashutosh Gowariker's *Lagaan*, Mira Nair's *Vanity Fair*, and Farhan Akhtar's *Dil Chahta Hai* and *Lakshya*. Working as an AD was a stepping stone, and Kagti, first and foremost an enthusiastic storyteller (even as a kid, she wrote for children's comic magazines), readied her script for her directorial debut, *Honeymoon Travels Pvt. Ltd.*

Excel Entertainment (the film studio owned by Farhan Akhtar and Ritesh Sidhwani) bought the rights to Kagti's script, and she proceeded to direct *Honeymoon Travels Pvt. Ltd.*, which was released in 2007. The idea for the plot originated with Reema's quirky take on a honeymooning couple who, unknown to each other, are real-life superheroes. A comic caper, the film traces the stories of six couples travelling to Goa on a honeymoon package tour, and delves into their singular *moments* of discovery and consequent coming to terms with each other. The film, starring eminent actors such as Shabana Azmi, Boman Irani and Abhay Deol, received a warm response from viewers, but more importantly, made evident Kagti's offbeat dramatic proclivity. However, the plain-spoken filmmaker has always been clear that *content*, to a great degree, is determined by commerce, even as she continues to redefine the parameters of commercial cinema.

Next, Kagti co-wrote *Zindagi Na Milegi Dobara* (ZNMD) in 2011 with Zoya Akhtar. It was only in 2012 that Kagti's second film, *Taalash*, produced by Excel Entertainment and Aamir Khan Productions, saw the light of the day. Starring Aamir Khan, Rani Mukherji and Kareena Kapoor, the film is a suspense drama examining the emotional turmoil of its lead characters, and, uncharacteristically, for Hindi films of the thriller genre, it is a psychological struggle that drives the riveting plot. Inspector Surjan Singh (Aamir Khan) aided by a local prostitute, Rosie (Kareena Kapoor), attempts to solve the mysterious death of a film star, further unravelling a series of noirish twists and turns. The film reaped commercial and critical success, and established the fact that Reema Kagti had arrived.

Reema Kagti

Galvanized by engaging stories, Kagti belongs to a new breed of filmmakers who are hammering away at an alternative cinema, tackling new subjects and adopting new modes of seeing. They reject labels of all kinds; the impatient Kagti shrugs off the gender label as being irrelevant and decisively outmoded. She is not a woman filmmaker; rather, she is an artist driven by stories, seeking the creative liberty to create a new vocabulary for Indian cinema.

Collaboration and Commerce— Treading the Thin Line

Preeti: *Tell us about your early life in Assam and your family.*

Reema: I was born in Assam. Most of my growing years were spent in a boarding school in Shillong and then in Delhi. I have two sisters. I lost my dad last year, but until his death he lived in Assam. My mother's still based there. My dad had a farm in a small village called Borhapjan. That was home to me while I was growing up. This area is in upper Assam, a very remote place to people from this part of the world. Initially, my dad worked in IndianOil Corporation Ltd.; he then gave up that job and started this little farm. It was just a piece of land with 12 anthills and he, in his lifetime, converted it into a tea-plantation — throughout my growing years, there were all kinds of schemes going on in the farm. There were all kinds of animals, different plantations and a lot of experimenting. My mother was a school teacher, but when we moved to the farm, she started doing fabric painting. She had an on-the-move kind of boutique. I had a very simple, middle-class upbringing with clichéd, good, God-fearing parents.

After the boarding school in Shillong, Loreto Convent, I went to DPS in Delhi. I was there till class 10. In the Northeast, there is a lack of educational institutions, and it's very normal for children to go to boarding school.

In the rest of the country, only naughty children are sent to boarding school, but in the Northeast, it's more of a necessity. There are some good schools in Guwahati and in Dibrugarh. Initially, I did go to Shillong, but I grew up in a small village and there weren't many options. My younger sister went to a school that was about two hours away from home, but that kind of travel for a kid was very taxing .... Why the Northeast is so underdeveloped, I don't know. Actually, it has to do with overall development. If you compare the Northeast with the rest of the country, the difference is quite stark.

We would go home for holidays. My dad loved nature, and we'd go for picnics and camping trips. We'd go to national parks such as Kaziranga and Manas.

Preeti: *What was the culture at home? Were your parents liberal or conservative?*

Reema: Both my parents came from pretty conservative set ups. Firstly, we were three girls, and there was no boy around.... From a very early age, we were always told that we had to grow up, work and be independent. So it was not a choice.

Nirmal: *Was there any opposition from your family when you joined films?*

Reema: Yes, there was, but you also have to understand that it was the eighties and Hindi cinema had really taken a downslide. So when in the nineties I expressed a desire to join films, my father was shocked. He said, 'I have educated you and I really want you to live a dignified life'. From his point of view Hindi cinema did not offer that. My mother's father had, back in those days, dabbled in some filmmaking in Assam, but nobody thought that it could be a real career option when I first suggested it. I was very insistent, and, in that sense, my parents have always been very supportive.

Preeti: *What was your equation with your sisters?*

Reema: My elder sister is just about two years older; so obviously, our experiences are very similar, as opposed to the younger one, who's about seven-and-a-half or eight years younger to me. But I am still very close to both of them. The younger one is, in fact, in Bombay now. My elder sister is in Bangalore. With my elder sister, it was a typical sibling relationship. Recently, she was complaining to me about her children who were fighting — one was trying to bite the other (they're about one and two). I had to remind her that we were around 12 by the time we stopped hitting each other! My mum used to separate us all the time.

Preeti: *Was Assam politically disturbed when you were growing up?*

Reema: You know, I saw it happening in my lifetime. I remember things were different before we moved to the farm. I was born in a town called Digboi, which was actually the oldest oil refinery in Asia, and where my dad worked in IndianOil. We used to live in these bungalows with glass doors and windows, and as a child, I remember, very often we wouldn't shut the doors. It was that safe. We would just go to sleep. When I was around 8 or 10, I became aware of the Assam Agitation. Now you have grills around houses, guards and all kinds of security, and you're still not safe.

Nirmal: *Did it affect you and your family?*

Reema: Of course, it did. Last year, my father finally sold the farm. Anyone who tries to do business or run something when there's this kind of a problem is headed for trouble.

Even people who are innocent are being treated horribly. People are being extorted—people have walked into my parents' house with AK-47s at nine in the night demanding money. If you pay up the extortionists then others say you are supporting them. If there's this kind of problem in the Northeast, it's also because people have been forsaken. There's a lot of problem in all states in the Northeast. Every two miles, there's a new group and some new organization. Some of them are political and some of them are terrorist outfits.

Nirmal: *Did your family watch films regularly?*

Reema: No, not really. I was a film buff. Nobody else really wanted to watch films, so I was constantly sent with the *ayah* or the *mali*.

Nirmal: *What kind of films did you like then? Was it stuff like world cinema?*

Reema: When you grow up in the Northeast, you're not exposed to the cream of anything. To a huge extent, I think I'm a product of piracy because that's what we got there. I watched mostly Hindi cinema. I was obsessed with Mr Bachchan. I loved all his films and I don't know why but *Mr. Natwarlal* was my favourite. I basically grew up on regular Hindi films released in the theatre. In Digboi, where we grew up, there was a club. On Saturdays and Sundays, there would be movie screenings in the club. There would be some Hollywood films also. But it was all pretty run-of-the-mill commercial stuff. I didn't have access to anything else.

I remember bunking school and going for *Salaam Bombay* at Chanakyapuri in Delhi. I shifted from Shillong to Delhi when I was in class 7. From class 7 to 10 I was in Delhi and then I moved to Bombay for junior college.

Nirmal: Was it a cultural shock coming from a beautiful place like Shillong to Delhi?

Reema: On one level it was, but I was in boarding school, so there were a lot of people like myself.

Preeti: I remember coming to Delhi University and feeling that Delhi had this bully culture, which makes assimilation tougher. Was it like that in school as well?

Reema: Not really. There was a very big hostel in R.K. Puram with a lot of kids from all over the place—from the Northeast and also some NRI kids.

Preeti: What kind of a student were you? Were you academically inclined?

Reema: I was okay academically, though I was not academically inclined. I used to play a lot of basketball.

Preeti: Were you ever a competitive student with mainstream carrier choices?

Reema: No, never. For a while, I wanted to be a journalist. When I moved to Bombay to Sophia for junior college (class 11), I joined the film club. That's where I first started seeing world cinema and stuff that I had never been exposed to.

   I didn't stay in Delhi for my junior college, even though my father wanted me to continue because even though I hadn't vocalized it, in my head, this film plan had already germinated. I wanted to come to Bombay. Though, to be honest, it was not some career move. My elder sister was studying here already. In Delhi, 11th and 12th were still school, and here in Bombay, it was college; so that had a lot to do with my wanting to shift. I just wanted as much freedom as I could get.

Nirmal: *Mumbai is a difficult city. But did coming to Mumbai open some windows for you?*

Reema: Yes, it is a difficult city. Even though I was in Delhi, I was quite protected because that's how it is in school. You can't just go wherever you want to. So for me it was a bit like coming from a small town to a really big city. I made a bunch of really good friends in college. It was good fun.

In the first year of junior college, I joined the film club and I got a lot of exposure to avant-garde Italian cinema, to Kurosawa and, you know, the classics. Though I didn't vocalize it back then, I don't think I was doing anything else. Once I started watching all these films, without me making too much of a big thing about it, I was already committed and moving towards films.

The first film that made a real impact was *Salaam Bombay*. I had been exposed to only commercial Hindi cinema, and it was for the first time that I watched something that was alternative. You don't know what clicks when in a human brain. For me, the moment when I decided I could do this was *Salaam Bombay*. There were no Indian films like that in the eighties.

Nirmal: *You didn't go through a film school or a course in film studies.*

Reema: I only did a one-year course in Sophia Polytechnic, which was like a course in social media communications and it covered everything. It covered journalism, PR, advertising, television and film. I tried to get into FTII four years in a row, got rejected and then stopped trying.

Preeti: *Why did you do a degree in literature?*

Reema: I love literature; I guess it was just that. I don't remember much about college because I was focusing too much on partying, watching movies and doing odd-end jobs such as writing articles and making a bit of money. Frankly, I cannot tell you what my course was about because it's the fun that I remember.

But, of course, I love reading books. I like reading fiction—from Shakespeare to John Grisham. You give me a good book and I'll read it. You give me a good film and I'll see it. With non-fiction it depends; there are some books that I have liked.

Preeti: *So then college wasn't really a ground for political mentoring? You didn't really have an ideology, so to speak, by then?*

Reema: Not really, and I think that my ways in college might have contributed to it.

Nirmal: *You like to read. Does storytelling come from that because cinema/mass media is the best kind of storytelling?*

Reema: I would always write. Even as a kid I wrote I used to send my stories to *Tinkle*. In fact, somebody found that out a couple of years ago, and it became a big joke. Uncle Pai would accept the stories and send ₹25 in the mail, like a cheque. So I was always a writer. As a child, I remember writing plays and then we would ask a couple of the neighbours' kids to act them out and sell tickets. Those are the kind of things that I did for fun and they came naturally.

Nirmal: *How did you make the transition to filmmaking because it's completely different from writing?*

Reema: I clearly knew that I wanted to write. I always knew that I'd write books or do journalism, but I was always a film buff too. Sometime later, when I was in junior college, I just felt a connection with films.

When I was watching *Salaam Bombay*, I remember thinking to myself that maybe I should do this.

Nirmal: *For a debut film,* Honeymoon Travels Pvt. Ltd. *was a risky proposition. It is neither an art film nor a complete commercial masala film. Were you aware of the risk?*

Reema: Yes, definitely. With *Honeymoon Travels Pvt. Ltd.*, only at the time of the release, when we put out the promos and distributors started buying the film, that it started to turn. But for Ritesh, Farhan and me, it was always an underdog project. Films are almost like people, you just don't know....

Nirmal: *An English-titled film will not have as many takers amongst the masses. It is an unlikely title. In* Honeymoon Travels Pvt. Ltd. *you had no major star. To use an English title is a risky proposition. Were you convinced about its commercial viability, or did you want to take a chance and make a debut film?*

Reema: The film was an unusual film, and I wanted to name it so that it would pique your interest. What is *Honeymoon Travels Pvt. Ltd.*? You see it on buses all the time; there's *Private Limited* written on them and that's where it came from.

I really felt it was an apt title. It is quirky and tells the audience what the film is about; basically, it's about honeymoon package tours.

I believed it (*Honeymoon Travels Pvt. Ltd.*) was commercially viable. I believed that about *Talaash* too. Today, because Aamir Khan has done it, it has suddenly turned on its head. Don't forget, I spent five years trying to make it. Apart from Farhan and Ritesh, nobody else thought it was a commercial proposition. So perception can change, and in today's filmmaking world, more than commercial and art cinema, you need to be viable.

Source: Authors.

Nirmal: *What makes it viable? If I were a distributor, I would think* – Honeymoon Travels Pvt. Ltd. – *would this film work?*

Reema: But distributors go by the audience's reaction to the promos. If there's a buzz when the promos come out, they know whether people want to see the film or not. On that level, *Honeymoon Travels Pvt. Ltd.* was a bit of an underdog till the promotions started. *Talaash* was an underdog film till we cast Aamir. Films are like that.

Preeti: *So by the end of college, you were clear in your mind that you wanted to get into filmmaking. How did you get into the industry?*

Reema: By the time I got out of college, I was already clear that I wanted to make films. When I was doing that one-year course, I had to also do an internship at the end. I was assigned to a television house, and so I went and spoke to my faculty and told them that I was really interested in films. I asked my faculty if I they would mind if I looked for a job in film industry myself because they didn't know anyone in films. I went and met Rajat Kapoor. He gave me a job. I started working on his first film, which was *Private Detective: Two Plus Two Plus One*. That was where I learned the basics of filmmaking. I worked as an AD. Rajat encouraged me to write. He was writing, and he would make me write with him. He directed me to write film scripts. Before that I was just writing short stories and novels. Under Rajat's influence, I first tried writing a film script. Also, it was a very small and low-budget film, so I worked with him as an AD. I helped with editing and assisted Rasul with the sound. That film was my training ground, and not so much college. I always like to say that my DVD player is my film school.

Preeti: *As an AD, financially, was it easy to survive in a city like Bombay?*

Reema: I was making good money as an AD. First ADs get paid reasonably well. The transition is difficult because you want to stop ADing. You feel that if you continue doing just that then people may not take you seriously as a director. At some point, you have to stop being an AD, which is when I started writing a bit for television.

I worked as an AD for *Private Detective: Two Plus Two Plus One, Bombay Boys, Lagaan, Dil Chahta Hai, Lakshya, Armaan....*

Preeti: *How did* Lagaan *happen?*

Reema: I had worked on *Bombay Boys* as the third AD with Apoorva Lakhia, who was the first AD to that film. So when he was hired to do *Lagaan*, he brought me in as a second AD.

Nirmal: *Did you realize that* Lagaan *would be such a blockbuster while making the film?*

Reema: I realized it while reading the script itself. It is about sports, nationalism.... it was a clear commercial hit even on paper.

Preeti: *What does an AD's work entail? Isn't it just hard labour?*

Reema: Traditionally in India there are 12–15 and everyone does everything. But when I started working, I worked with someone like Apoorva, who had worked on a couple of movies in America, and followed the first AD system — a system that most professionals in the world follow. There's a first AD, there's a second AD, and they liaison between the director and various other heads of departments (HODs).

Preeti: *What is the difference in work as third AD and as first AD?*

Reema: As a first AD, you are basically the head of the AD department. You schedule the film — it is your responsibility and not the director's — you take the director's and DP's inputs, and basically plan day-to-day shoot. You have a second AD on the set, planning the next day's shoot. You have seconds, who are handling cast and thirds, who are handling background. Amongst your AD department, you'll split up various people who'll liaise with different departments. As a third AD, you end up coordinating lock ups and working with background — running, cueing and doing background action on the set.

But you hardly move up. I was third AD on *Bombay Boys*, I was second on *Dil Chahta Hai* and then finally I became first AD on *Lakshya*.

Preeti: *Is there a norm in the industry that you will take a certain time to graduate from AD to director?*

Reema: Not in our industry but everywhere else, where there are unionized industries, whether in America or England, you have to clock a number of hours as a set performance audit to become an AD. Then you need to clock a certain number of hours to go from third AD to second AD. In India, whatever work is happening, everything is lawless.

In the last 5–6 years, the film industry has really grown, both in terms of width and depth. There is the multiplex audience. You know, a Hindi film with an English title and a small, unknown cast would have been a very risky project, had there been just a single screen. The success of *Honeymoon Travels Pvt. Ltd.* was that it was the first of the medium-budget films that didn't have a big cast, but recovered its cost. It was unheard of for a film to even do that or be marketed abroad. It did very well abroad. But films that were without a star cast were not explored in these kinds of markets. That's what Ritesh and Farhan did and made it a success.

Preeti: *How fair is the industry in terms of giving a chance to real talent? Does everybody who is good get his due or is it more to do with luck?*

Reema: Luck has something to do with it. I do know people who have been waiting for years to do their films. I don't know why that happens. It's really hard to say. It's like any other industry where you decide to do something; not everyone is successful. Maybe the project is not right or you're not suited to do this. Sometimes, it's just plain bad luck.

Nirmal: *When you started making your film, you were a woman with her debut. Did you experience resistance from your technicians or your crew members? Did you face trouble from the financers/producers or the star cast?*

Reema: No, not at all. I had a great star cast. In fact, I was the most junior member of the entire cast and crew. Everybody was sweet and really supportive.

But personally, I feel that the Hindi film industry is very secular; they don't care which religion you belong to. Also, now with so many women coming into the industry, at least with the crew I have worked with, I have never had a bad experience—I started when I was 24 and now I'm 40, though there are many people with horror stories. Even, say, guys who you normally would not be comfortable mixing with—all the light boys and spot boys—they are my buddies, and they are very *pahuncha hua* in terms of their attitude towards women. There's a lot of good stuff, but there's bad stuff too like in every situation. You have to look at both ends of the spectrum. Yes, the bad can get bad, but the good is very good.

Nirmal: *One thing that comes to my mind is that didn't an actor like Boman Irani, who is also a photographer/technician interfere in the photography department?*

Reema: No. On the set, he's completely focused on being an actor and trying different stuff. I know he's a photographer, but on the set, he is a very involved and enthusiastic actor.

Preeti: *When did you start writing* Honeymoon Travels Pvt. Ltd.*?*

Reema: I got off *Lakshya* and I had written a kind of short story about the superhero couple. Throughout the shooting of *Lakshya*, up in the mountains of Ladakh, this was going on in my head. I thought it's crazy to do a film on two superheroes, you know, it's not real. But I really wanted to do it because there was something I was trying to say through that short story. The story basically was that nobody is perfect, and no couple is perfect. These guys are perfect because they are superheroes. I was obsessed with that story. Up in the mountains, one day it came to me that I should build it up, bring more people to it and bring real couples around them to bring out this point. My parents had gone to Shimla on a typical middle-class honeymoon when they got married, and my dad was a kind of bungling character, and a lot of things went wrong, like my mother got lost because he left her somewhere. It was not your typical honeymoon story; it was more like a honeymoon had gone wrong. I've grown up with these stories and that's where the idea came from.

You don't know what meshes with what. I, myself, am constantly amazed at the kind of things that come up when and where you put things in. Whether I was writing *Honeymoon Travels Pvt. Ltd.* or *ZNMD*, there are so many things that happen that are so clearly unrelated. Twenty-two years later, you remember something and you connect it together in a script. It's hard to really kind of follow it.

Preeti: *Did you decide to take a writing break, or did you do it alongside everything else?*

Reema: I took some time out, about three or four months, and wrote it. Then I was going around looking for producers, trying to cast it.

Preeti: *How difficult was it to find a producer for this subject?*

Reema: This one was easy because the minute I went out with it, there was this production house that picked me up. I worked with them for about six months, but it didn't work out. By that time, Farhan and Ritesh had also told me that if it didn't work out then I could go to them because they liked the film. So when the first deal didn't work out, I went to them... and from start to its release it was two years.

Preeti: *When you were writing the script, were you pretty clear that you would be directing it too?*

Reema: I was writing for me to make a film. Before this also I had written another script, which didn't happen; so this was my second attempt. When I did first take it around there were a couple of people who said that they'd like to buy the script. But I said no, it's a package deal, I come with the script. I was writing it as a platform for myself.

Preeti: *Was it difficult to put together an ensemble cast in your first project itself and have so many people to direct? Was it a challenge?*

Reema: Ignorance is bliss. I had never directed anything. All I had done was a four-minute video film with eight of us together. Though I had worked as an AD and had a very good vantage point as to how films were directed, I didn't have any hands-on experience.

Also, it's not like I had decided that I was going to make an ensemble film. I was trying to do something creative and then it became an ensemble film. I just tried to do as a director what was right by the script.

Nirmal: *When you came to the set for the first time, how was the feeling of calling out the first cut? From an AD, you had become the boss on the set.*

Reema: Great. It was the first shot and I was a bit stressed out. The first shot finished and I turned around, and there were all my best friends like Zoya and Ayan working with me on the film and they were all crying. The same thing happened at Zoya's first shot because for us, it had taken so long. So that's what I told her — other girls cry at their weddings and we cry at our first shots.

Nirmal: *I would have thought that if I had to make a film, I'd start from the word 'go', but it never happens.*

Reema: See, it's not practical to go chronologically. Supposing it takes time to get to a particular location and get out of it, and supposing this is my main character's house — in terms of the story, he might be seen at that location right now, then in scene 30 and then in scene 65. But if we keep going in and out of a place trying to shoot chronologically, the amount of money wasted, and the time... it takes very long.

Preeti: *All this requires a lot of project planning.*

Reema: That's what a first AD does. That is what actually scheduling is called. It depends because different people work differently. I would like a first AD to do my scheduling.

Nirmal: *But doesn't it hamper your creativity as a director because after all you have written the script as well?*

Preeti: *Besides, it also requires a great deal of detachment.*

Reema: But also, you do rehearsals and you do readings of the cast, so everybody is on the same page. I know from the outside it looks like *Oh! you're just jumping sections*, but there is a method to the madness. It's the job of the ADs and the director to communicate to people what's happening.

Preeti: *Did you also do the screenplay of* Honeymoon Travels Pvt. Ltd.*?*

Reema: I wrote it and Anurag did the dialogues.

Preeti: *What is the difference between a script and a screenplay, and does the same person end up doing it all?*

Reema: Zoya and I, we write the script and screenplay. We write the screenplay, write the dialogues in English and then get someone to translate them in Hindi because my Hindi is clearly not up to the mark. In Delhi, the only thing that I couldn't grapple with was Hindi. It was easier for me to pass German than Hindi. Being from the Northeast, Hindi was never a priority.

To my mind, a script and a screenplay are the same thing.

Nirmal: *What was the process for deciding the cast of the film? Were the actors that you cast your first choices?*

Reema: You have to juggle a lot. It's also getting everybody's group dates together, so we lost a lot of people because we didn't have dates. A lot of people were my first choices.

Nirmal: *Shabana, a seasoned actor, seems a bit of an odd choice for this kind of a movie. Didn't you think of other actors?*

Reema: Shabana, weirdly for me, was always the first choice for this role. I wasn't so confident that she would say yes, but I knew that it would be great if she did it.

Nirmal: *Since you were also the scriptwriter along with being the director, there would have been an image of each character in your mind. Initially, I felt that for Boman's character, Anupam Kher would have been better. But then I thought that Boman has done a beautiful job. Did you have this kind of doubt regarding the star cast?*

Reema: No.

Nirmal: Everything went on as expected?

Reema: It's basically Murphy's Law. Everything that can go wrong will go wrong. It's never a smooth journey.

Preeti: In our minds, as the audience or critics, we have formed a certain coterie of directors, such as you, Dibakar, Anurag, Sagar. While we were talking to Tigmanshu, he said that he aspired to make a mainstream, masala movie and wondered why we were slotting him in this category. He said that given a chance, main toh banaoonga, kyon nahin banaoonga. I was telling him that I liked the fact that there weren't unnecessary songs, etc., in Paan Singh Tomar, to which he replied that he would love to put songs in his movies and asked me what was wrong with that. We were talking about the evolution in the cinema that he made, from Haasil to Paan Singh Tomar. But he did not look at it in those terms, and he was very unapologetic about it.

The classification of films is what I'm talking about – do you think it is very arbitrary and doesn't actually exist?

Reema: I do think so. I feel that all kinds of classification on a level are very reductionist. People ask me the *women question* all the time, to the point, where I am like, *bhaiya* please don't. I don't answer reporters who suddenly slide in something and I say that I can't answer this, but they'll write your answer anyway. It's not about good or bad classification. By saying that somebody is alternative or somebody is commercial, on a level, you're reducing it. If you see the new, emerging films that are doing well, they've got a foot in both sides. You take *ZNMD*, which technically is such a commercial film, but again it was another underdog film. The day before it released, it was touted as possibly the year's biggest flop. But that's not how it worked out. To me, the film comes from a very commercial space, but what it's saying is spiritual. It's not just about holidaying and partying.

Nirmal: ZNMD *is a fantastic film, but if I were the financer I would have wanted an established heroine starring against major heroes. Kalki was a newer face. You had an opportunity with Hrithik Roshan and Farhan Akhtar. You could have got any female lead.*

Reema: But Zoya wanted Kalki and thought she was the best person. I thought Kalki did a great job.

Nirmal: Of course, looking at the film one agrees with you. But if I were the financer, I would have wanted a more bankable name.

Reema: That's where Ritesh and Farhan come into play as producers. They don't do this kind of thing. They don't do something just because it's bankable.

Nirmal: Days have changed.

Reema: I think people change days. You have people who think differently. Nowadays, there's a market for any kind of film. Ten years ago, it wasn't so. Today, you can be any kind of a filmmaker and hope to have a career in India. Ten or twenty years ago, if you were an alternate filmmaker… there was no scene, it was not alive. You'd be you in isolation making films.

Nirmal: When you watch other filmmakers, how do you react? What catches your fancy?

Reema: I am a film buff. I watch a film a day on DVD. I go to the theatre also. I average about five or six films a week. There are so many films to watch in the world.

Sometimes you read about a film, and sometimes there's a director that you love and follow.

Nirmal: *How do you rate critics? I find some of them very biased and ill informed.*

Reema: On the whole, and I'm not speaking about one person specifically, I feel that this entire business of film criticism in India is quite appalling. They give their personal opinions, whereas they are supposed to be showing the film in perspective to the audience. I do think, by and large, and I'm not taking any names, it's like if the critics give bad reviews then I go and watch that film.

Nirmal: *We have a film club in our college, but we hardly find any takers for the film critique course. You need to have student training at college level to learn and understand films. The transition from film appreciation to film criticism doesn't happen.*

Reema: But what I'm saying is that the beauty of cinema is in the fact that you don't need any training to enjoy a film.

Preeti: *I don't think that the critics pan a movie because it's not good or maybe they are just plain dumb, but if you are giving four stars to* Rowdy Rathore *and giving a two-and-a-half or a cautious three to* Paan Singh Tomar *then I have serious concerns regarding your motives.*

Reema: For me, I personally feel our audience has way more brains than any of the critics. Whenever I have a live session with an audience, I'm amazed because when you're in the industry, you're constantly being told that you have to dumb it down for the audience, but when I have personal interactions with them I really feel that it's not true. This new, emerging multiplex audience is giving my life meaning because I can make the films I want to.

Nirmal: *I am a person with limited income and I have two children. If I take two children, my wife and a nephew who stays with me – five people, when we go to a cinema hall, it costs me*

₹2,000 to ₹3,000 with popcorn, etc. thrown in. So I would like to know about the film. They write such random reviews that when you go to the film you realize that actually the film is good.

Reema: Yes that happens, but I feel that you also have to discern, which is why there is publicity. You can also look at the promos of a film and decide whether you want to give it a chance. Sometimes, critics give it a good review and people go to watch it, but word of mouth is bad and eventually the film does badly. Sometimes, critics give a bad review, but word of mouth is very good — what we've just seen with *Gangs of Wasseypur*. Critics had panned it, but word of mouth was good and the public liked it. I think it's a huge success. You can't look at everything in terms of 100–150 crores. You have to look at the attempt and how far the attempt is also going. To me, it's one of the biggest successes of the year.

Nirmal: How do you react to such people? How do you react when people don't write good things about your films and your work?

Reema: I just say, what do they know and I move on! You can't make everybody happy.

Source: Authors.

Director and screenwriter Zoya Akhtar comes from a prestigious lineage of film artists. Her grandfather, Jan Nisar Akhtar, a prominent Urdu poet of the Progressive Writers' Movement and recipient of the Sahitya Akademi Award, was also a respected lyricist in Bollywood. Zoya is the daughter of celebrated Urdu lyricist, scriptwriter and poet Javed Akhtar and child actor-turned-prolific screenwriter Honey Irani. Akhtar's childhood was spent around the bigwigs of the film fraternity, and she and her brother, Farhan, became incidental observers of the nitty-gritty of scriptwriting and of the mechanics of filmmaking as a whole.

With cinema, rather than blood, coursing through her veins, Bollywood would have been the indisputable career choice, but Akhtar had other plans. A degree in law or journalism was more to her liking especially since Hindi cinema of the late eighties and nineties struck her as dull and uninspiring. It was Mira Nair's award-winning, gritty docudrama *Salaam Bombay* (1988), which convinced Akhtar that other forms of cinema were possible and that the business of filmmaking was one to aspire to. Zoya earned her Bachelor of Arts from St. Xavier's College in Mumbai. She also worked as an advertising copywriter while pursuing her degree.

Akhtar's first assignment was as a casting director for Mira Nair's *Kama Sutra* (1996). She even bagged a bitsy role in the film as one of Rekha's (teacher of the *Kama Sutra*) disciples. Zoya also worked as a casting director for Kaizad Gustad's *Bombay Boys* (1998) and Dev Benegal's *Split Wide Open* (1999). She then completed a course on film production from New York University. Akhtar had written the script for her first film, *Luck by Chance*, but owing to casting difficulties, she put it on the back burner. In the meantime, her brother Farhan Akhtar was making his first film, *Dil Chahta Hai* (2001), and Zoya acted as a first assistant as well as a casting director on the set. She also assisted Farhan with *Lakshya* (2004), and was the co-writer and the executive producer for her good friend Reema Kagti's directorial debut, *Honeymoon Travels Pvt. Ltd.* (2007).

After a wait of almost six years, Akhtar resumed work on *Luck by Chance* in 2008, and it was finally ready for release in 2009. The film had Farhan Akhtar and Konkona Sen in the lead roles, along with the stars of yesteryears, Rishi Kapoor and Dimple Kapadia. The plot revolves around the persistent Vikram Jaisingh, who is hell-bent on making it big in the film industry, and young starlet Sona Mishra who, though ambitious, is not without scruples. The story traces the development of these two characters as it also examines the trappings of the Hindi film world. Attempting to recreate the ambience of the film industry, a host of Bollywood heavyweights, parading as their own selves, made cameo appearances in the film.

Akhtar's *Luck by Chance* received a middling response from the audience, but the critics were more than generous, and many felt that this was one of the few films that provided an honest and reflexive representation of the film industry.

2011 saw the release of Akhtar's second film, *ZNMD*, a cinematic extravaganza set in Spain. Zoya roped in an interesting mix of actors—superstars Hrithik Roshan and Katrina Kaif, and alternative cinema's favourites, Kalki Koechlin and Abhay Deol, for the film. *ZNMD* is not only a classic road trip, but also, like all road trips, a journey that entails rediscovering cast-away selves and estranged friendships. The story follows three best friends on a holiday and how each one of them negotiates life's disappointments, but more importantly, how they then experience collective moments of epiphany. The film was a resounding success, both critically and commercially, and not just in India but overseas as well. Zoya Akhtar, the filmmaker, was here to stay.

Zoya's most recent offering is a short film, *Sheila ki Jawaani*, as part of a collection of four shots directed by four influential filmmakers. The film depicts the bitter-sweet tale of a young boy, Vicky, who prefers dancing to cricket and worships Katrina Kaif. Akhtar and Reema Kagti had written this story years back with the legend Helen in mind. When the opportunity presented itself, Zoya decided to direct this story and made it current by introducing Sheila (Katrina Kaif) in the narrative.

Zoya Akhtar has found her place within the league of contemporary directors who are carving a new form of Indian cinema, inventive and relevant, and the one that is constantly reimagining the craft of making movies.

Urban and Unapologetic— The Cinema of Zoya Akhtar

Preeti: *What sets you apart from all the filmmakers we have interviewed so far is that you come from an industry family. What was it like growing up in the thick of Bollywood?*

Zoya: I grew up in a family that was into films. My mother was an actress; she was a child star. My father was a writer. They hooked up during a movie that he had written and she was acting in called *Seeta Aur Geeta*. That's when they got married. I was born when she was 18 and my father was 25 or 26. So they were very young parents, and a year later my brother was born. My mother stopped working for a while when we were born and then decided that she wanted to make films. She was an AD and then went to FTII—so we used to go there for the weekends. I was always surrounded by films. We had crew and cast in the house, as well as screenings, discussions. My father and Salim were writing, so we were always privy to their discussions. My mother used to have a projector, so we used to get prints from the theatre and watch films.

Preeti: *So was it a natural choice to get into filmmaking, or were there other alternatives that you were also considering?*

Zoya: I mean you are just exposed to it a lot. When I got into college, it was 1988... and when you are a kid you like everything, it's all entertaining, but after a point, when you're 12 or 13, you're a little more discerning and the films then were awful, at least Hindi films were at that point. So I never thought that this was something I would do. When I got into Xavier's, I really contemplated whether it would be law, journalism or advertising.

Preeti: *Were you a very good student?*

Zoya: Not at all. I wasn't bad, but I just didn't study as much. I was always like a student with 70%, and I got 72% in my 10th grade. I wasn't one of the toppers. I was average. But there were subjects that I liked, and I was very good at like English or Math. But I wasn't studying to top ever and the environment wasn't such that we were asked to either. There was no pressure on us. We just had to do ok in subjects we were good at and pass in subjects we weren't good at. That was it. We weren't forced to come first.

Law and journalism interested me. I've always been a reader. Also, advertising was hip at that time. The people that were in advertising were also educated and well read, and it was considered more creative because you had those dirty, horrid blockbusters, and they were awful. Then I was in Xavier's, and I saw *Salaam Bombay*. That was it. I just knew I wanted to make movies.

I started copywriting when I was still in college and was 19. At that time, I was pursuing arts, and majored in sociology and literature. So I started working when I was 19, freelancing with a place called the Script Shop, with a writer called Adi Pocha. I started writing and he taught me a lot; basically, discipline, getting down there, sitting down till it came. He taught me a lot on the craft of it.

Then I got a weird phone call one day from a casting director called Uma da Cunha who was casting a film called *Kama Sutra*, and it was weird because it was Mira Nair, and *Salaam Bombay* was an iconic film for me. They said they wanted to screen test me. I told them that I wasn't an actress and that I couldn't act. They said that she wanted to meet me, and I said ok. They sent me the lines, I learnt the lines and so I went to do a screen test for Mira. I'm sure I was awful — she never talks about it, but I told her that I really wanted to work with her. She asked me to send her some of my work. I sent her my work and she hired me. I was one of the assistants for *Kama Sutra* and started working with casting. I was the basic runner, working with background action on the set, so you can call me the third AD. I was on the set most of the time. That was the first film that I did and it was amazing. Then I started working on movies.

Preeti: *What happened after* Kama Sutra*?*

Zoya: Then I worked with Dev Benegal for *Split Wide Open* and then with Kaizad Gustad for *Bombay Boys*. I went to New York and did a course in film production at New York University, which was a great fun. It was good because I had already worked in the business, so I had a bit of an edge.

Nirmal: *You were already in the industry. Why did you do a course in film production? You would have known everything by then.*

Zoya: It is always good to learn theory. It's good fun — you have a camera, you're shooting and living in New York — it's a blast. I don't regret it. I had done a diploma, but I wish I'd done a degree. It was a six-month programme. It helps because you just watch films, you learn film theory and no one teaches you that practically, and you also see and do so much work where you're encouraged to develop your own skill. A lot of people who want to go into films don't know what to do. You figure out what you want to specialize in. In my case, though, I knew I wanted to direct, even before

I went there. It was awesome. In fact, if I have any regret in life it's that I didn't go for longer.

The diploma course was a primary course where you had to learn everything. I had to learn about lighting even though I had no interest. They believed that tomorrow if you're doing a guerrilla film with five dollars, you should know how to light. It was like that I would have paid one dollar to somebody to do this stuff, but you had to do it. We had to write, we had to direct; it was very democratic. So you'd put in your concepts without your name and then everybody elected the script they liked the best. So the top five films got to be made. So, of course, I got to make my film.

Preeti: *Didn't you feel at that time that may be you'd want to stay back and explore their industry and other cinematic traditions? Or were you very clear that you had to return to India?*

Zoya: Yes, I had to come back because I was going to make Indian films, initially at least. So I came back and then worked with Farhan. I started writing my script and Farhan started making *Dil Chahta Hai*. So I was the first AD to him, I cast his film. I had written *Luck by Chance* but had been unable to cast it. So in the meantime, I executive produced *Lakshya* and *Honeymoon Travels Pvt. Ltd.* I wrote another script and then *Luck by Chance* happened.

Nirmal: *You were closely associated with* Dil Chahta Hai. *One thing that was written endlessly about it was that it was an unabashed celebration of wealth and the rich class, and that it was an ode to money. The characters were not ashamed of driving a Mercedes or going to exotic locales like Goa. Were you worried about the script at that time? The critics were positive, but they were also writing about it as the first film that celebrated wealth.*

Zoya: No, I was never worried.

What about Yash Chopra films and Karan Johar films? They only make films that celebrate wealth. *Kuch Kuch Hota Hai* had already been made.

Nirmal: *In both* Dil Chahta Hai *and* ZNMD, *there is money and a youngster wants to spend. These are very urban films.*

Zoya: In *ZNMD*, we have working men and professionals — one is a banker, one is working with his father in his business and one is a copywriter. These are people who have money and have the right to spend it however they want. We are talking about a certain profile that exists. I have been told a lot of this about *ZNMD*. That it's about people who have money. For me, either the characters resonate with you and the story resonates with you or they don't. The economic stratum of the characters of the film is really not my concern. I don't go to see *Gangs of Wasseypur* and then say, 'Oh God! They are poor,' and so I can't watch this film. What does it mean? Either it makes sense to me or it doesn't. I mean I don't believe in royalty, so should I not watch *Jodhaa Akbar* because they're royal characters? I don't think like that... whether this character has money or doesn't have money, or whether it is unabashed display of wealth.

In India, if you make *Slumdog Millionaire* you are celebrating poverty, if you're making films about money you are celebrating wealth — they just want to cry and complain. The question is — do you like the film or do you not like the film? Does this person's journey move you or doesn't it? How much money do they have in their bank balance in the movie — how is that your problem? That I don't understand. If you make films about poor people, you're told nobody wants to watch it because it's reality. I made *Luck by Chance*, which didn't have rich people in it, but nobody saw it. Why not? It's about struggling people. Why aren't you watching this film if you feel that we are not showing your life's struggle?

And I am very urban, so how can I make rural films? I mean I can try but... (laughs). I can make films that I know and stories that come from me. I mean, yes of course, I can make something else and I hope to be able to master my craft in a way that I can then go somewhere, research and develop a story, make it my own and tell it with as much finesse. But I think I'm still in that zone where things are personal and where I'm still coming from personal experience. I don't think I've developed to that space yet where I can go elsewhere.

Preeti: *Interestingly, if you look at the movies that are being made, for instance,* Paan Singh Tomar, Haasil *or* Gangs of Wasseypur, *the filmmakers are from that belt, that region. So they're not making something out of the blue — it is the milieu that they come from and they're making movies about that.*

Zoya: Precisely. If you go into ZNMD and the only thing you come out with is that these people are rich then I have failed. Then it's a problem.

Nirmal: *What goes through your mind when you have to decide a title for your film? How do you decide? Your first film was titled in English.*

Zoya: Nobody in the world — in the English-speaking world — uses the phrase *luck by chance*, except in Bombay. It is street colloquialism. It is only *Mumbaiya* language. So to me it's extremely Indian.

Preeti: *Why did you choose a subject like* Luck by Chance *for your first film?*

Zoya: I had many ideas, but this was the only idea that I saw through. I wasn't stuck with it — it just happened.

It was also very close to home. I've grown up in the industry, I've worked as an AD and so I knew all those characters. From the junior artist to the struggling actors to the artist suppliers to the ADs to the sound guys—I just know these people. I know them inside out and I've hung out with them. All the time, I hear their nonsense, I hear how it works and I know the stars. I was privy to all these people.

Also, the whole thing about success and failure—especially when you live in Bombay where everything is film-centric. It is really freaky. I can make *Luck by Chance*, and be considered a failure by industry insiders but somebody outside, say in Delhi, who wants to be a filmmaker might look at me and say I'm a success. So who decides this? It has to be a very individual choice. Am I doing okay or not? To me the fact that I made the film I wanted to is success. How many people eventually get to do what they want to do or even succeed at what they're doing? The definition of success in the industry is just ridiculous. You're constantly told whether you're successful or not. So I think it came from that and the fact what is personal success—thematically it came from that.

But also, there was this whole circus that needed to be portrayed. One more thing that I was told was that it was an insider's view of the industry.

Preeti: *But I feel that it was a very outsider's view.*

Zoya: I think so too.

Preeti: *For me, as a common person, that is the interesting part. Having been born and brought up in the industry, the overriding perspective that you bring to the story is that of Konkona's character. While Farhan's character is totally absorbed by the system, what really stands out is the fact that this woman manages to* *retain her dignity and hold her own – that's what I take back from the movie.*

Zoya: Yes, it's noble, and that's why you take it back. But his perspective to me is also important. After all she's also part of the system. Who's to say that he won't really grow a conscience? By the end of the film, he actually does. He does what he needs to do. He does this to get what he wants. He's not killing anyone. Yeah, so he's bullshitting two chicks with manipulating two women, but it's okay. He's done what he has to do, and he comes back and apologizes. She realizes that this is not the kind of person she wants to be with because he's probably going to be like that for the rest of his life. Fair enough. But I think people go back with her in mind not just because she's noble, but also because she assesses for herself. You also need to make that assessment for yourself when you don't get that big, massive break on a level as well. You kind of maintain your sanity.

So it's these two perspectives with both of them, and it's both their attitudes towards each other and life, and their self-esteem. I think your self-esteem really affects your destiny. I honestly believe how you view yourself affects where you reach. People either get ingratiating or cocky. She has this attitude that if it has to happen, it will happen, and she's waiting for this man very expectantly, and for him it's like, of course it's going to happen; we just have to figure out when and where is the opportunity coming up. Both these perspectives are important to me. But, of course, she's the Joan of Arc of the film – it starts with her and it ends with her. Also, she's the good one.

Preeti: *How long did it take you to write the script?*

Zoya: It took me three to four months. I wrote it in Goa on the beach. But then I worked on it a lot more. I hand-wrote it — I don't know why! I came back and it was an epic. So then I just hacked it. I just cut out characters, tracks. It was super fun, but it was huge. So it took me time.

Preeti: *When you started writing, what was it that you developed first? Was there a pin board and you decided on particular characters, or did you randomly start writing the script?*

Zoya: Not at all. *Luck by Chance* was the first picture that I wrote as a one-liner and then I fleshed out the scenes, I just kept writing and I didn't know what I was doing. I had no process.

Preeti: *Did you have a beginning or end in mind? Was there a notion of why you were writing this particular story?*

Zoya: Yes, of course you have to. I knew what the end was. I knew what was happening, but I was just tripping out and just going everywhere, putting everything into the film and every experience that I'd had that should have gone in, went in. There were various characters, and it was just too big. But then Reema (Kagti) and I started working together, and a process came into shape because we both came from writing alone, and our own crazy processes to come into what didn't work the last time. Now it's better. We wrote *Zindagi...* in three months.

Preeti: *It's difficult for me to understand how people can write stories together.*

Zoya: It starts with a lot of talking, research, and we etch out a beginning, middle and an end. We talk about characters. It doesn't matter who's punching it into the laptop, but we try and discuss and put a one-liner for every scene in the film.

Like if we had to write a screenplay, what would happen first? In one line, in this scene this could happen, where the father would meet the son and talk about this. Then we take the story all the way through.

Nirmal: *Did you improvize on the sets and tweak the screenplay as you went along?*

Zoya: No, not the screenplay. Maybe a couple of lines, maybe some dialogues, but never really a scene.

Nirmal: *What about the tomato festival scene in ZNMD?*

Zoya: We had to shoot that scene as it was, and it was just madness. Of course, we had researched Spain. We had already travelled, been there on a holiday to Barcelona for 10 days. Then when we started writing about Spain, we knew basically what Spain's stop-of-the-pops was. You have La Tomatina, you have running with the bulls and you have certain places that are a must-see, the beaches, etc. Then you see what you want to use and what you don't and where it fits, but you have research before you start writing.

The only scene that was improvized was the scene in the bar with the three male leads where he (Hrithik) starts saying that his mother tried to arrange his marriage. The joke was just that his mother tried to arrange his marriage. But it wasn't embarrassing enough. Because Hrithik was performing it, he said that he didn't find it embarrassing enough and said that we should do something else too. So, Farhan, Hrithik and I sat down and wrote that he got rejected. That was the only scene that was improvized on the set because it wasn't hitting the spot.

Preeti: *Whose idea was ZNMD?*

Zoya: My idea was that I wanted to do a road trip and I wanted to go to Mexico, so I thought that I might as well shoot a film there because when you're shooting, you

Zoya Akhtar

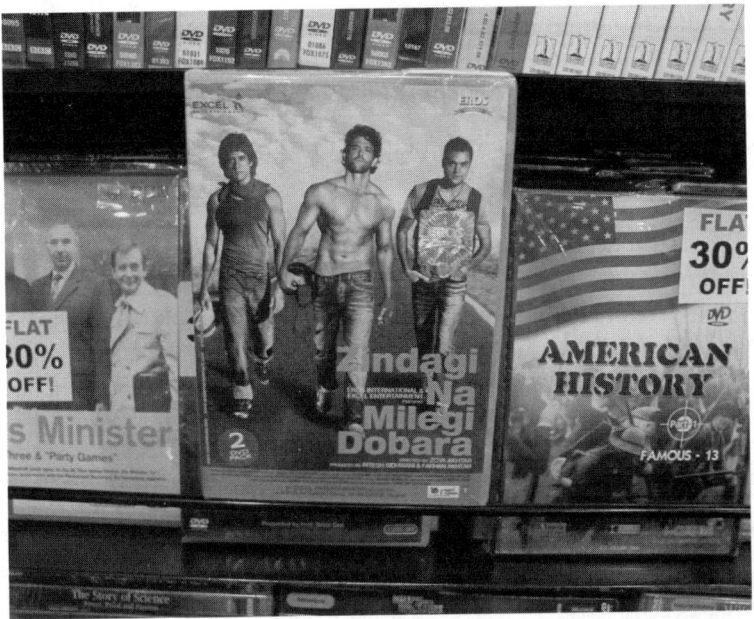

Source: Authors.

live there. I wanted to live and write in Mexico. Then we started developing it for Mexico. But we needed something to glue it together. Reema's (Kagti) friend had run with the bulls—these three girls had made a pact and gone running with the bulls.

Preeti: *Why didn't you choose female protagonists?*

Zoya: Because it would have been a slightly boring road trip. Also, we knew it was a big-budget film, and when you're making a film like this, at least in India, you should have actors if you want your film to see the light of the day.

I've been on road trips with women, and I've been on road trips with men—it's more cinematic with men. There's more I could have done as a director.

Preeti: *It's interesting you brought in Katrina's character in the capacity in which it is there. Even though it's a celebration of manhood, the catalyst remains the woman.*

Zoya: I think it's the emancipation of man. I think it is men freeing themselves.

Preeti: *Now everybody wants to go to Spain. It has really become a cult movie. I have seen so many friends uploading Facebook photo albums by the name* Zindagi Na Milegi Dobara. *They are doing everything that is being done in the film. Whether it's in Spain or New Zealand or elsewhere, the title of the photo albums remains synonymous with the movie.*

Zoya: It's not all about money. You can go to Ladakh and climb a mountain, or go to Rishikesh and white-water raft.

Preeti: *The other thing about ZNMD and* Dil Chata Hai *is the celebration of male bonding. I don't see those sorts of scripts coming on women. It is high time. Women are happening!*

Zoya: Yes, sure. Just look at Vidya Balan—she's totally happening. But where ZNMD was concerned, I don't know, I just wanted it to be more physical—the adventure, the physicality of it. Also, it's more interesting because men don't talk that much and they have a level of stupidity they can reach, which women can't reach ever. I never thought of doing it with women.

Nirmal: *Men without women have not really been explored. These films are an ode to those men who wish to be explored as themselves, and not only with reference to women. Throughout the movie Kalki's character is an intruder. Men of my age, in our late forties, freaked out because we never had this sort of thing.*

Preeti: *The film shows changing attitudes even where women, be it wife or girlfriend, are concerned. In the traditional Indian set up, Kalki's character, an overprotective, concerned girlfriend,* would have been shown in a sympathetic light, but here she is an intruder and not a desirable woman. That was a shift in perception. It was such a relief!

Nirmal: So why Kalki? You could have found anyone for this film.

Zoya: I like Kalki. Not everyone do that role. Most actresses wouldn't do that role with Katrina Kaif as the lead and then be the character that gets dumped! There are too many problems with actresses. And Kalki's a great actor and she looks great. She has a sense of humour. She had never played this kind of role and it was new for her. She's the polar opposite of this character. For her, it was so much fun to do this. She's sporting. I wouldn't get somebody of that calibre, who can look like her, who can perform as well for a role like this.

Nirmal: I was in Spain sometime back and spoke to the people at the Indian embassy there, and they said that they get a large number of enquiries, all thanks to ZNMD.

Zoya: Yes, I know. Spanish tourism came on board and they helped us with all the permissions all over the country, and also a certain amount of money was converted to marketing.

Nirmal: *Was it easy shooting in Spain?*

Zoya: Yes and no. They are very strict with rules and regulations, and they stick to timing, and we are the wild, wild, east. So, those things are tough. You can only shoot 12 hours. But it's all so good.

Preeti: *How do you balance while directing an ensemble cast or do you at all? Inevitably, for the audience, one person still emerges to be the hero. In* Dil Chahta Hai *it was Aamir Khan and in ZNMD, it ends up being Farhan Akhtar. If you talk to the* *general audience they feel Farhan is the hero, and not Hrithik. Is it a conscious decision or is it treatment of the characters or does it just happen?*

Zoya: I think, here the person who has the funniest lines becomes most popular. I needed Hrithik in the film. For one, I really like him and second, he's a star. So, he enables a certain budget. We'd written the role for Farhan. But I spoke to Farhan and told him that I was going to narrate the film to Hrithik, and what if Hrithik wanted to do Imran because Imran was actually written for Farhan. Farhan said that if he wanted to do Imran, let him do it. I didn't tell Hrithik which part I was pitching to him and he chose Arjun. I'm glad he did because he was very good with it. Also, it wouldn't work for the audience if the girl kind of dumped him and kissed Abhay Deol or Farhan. They wouldn't buy it. I love Abhay and Farhan to death, but it's the truth! The audience is bizarre. For example, there's a theatre where *Dilwale Dulhania Le Jayenge* has been running forever. My friend was doing a documentary and she went there and asked people why they were still watching the film. They said that it was for Shahrukh and Kajol's *jodi*. The people there say that Kajol should not have married Ajay Devgan. So, my friend said that Shahrukh was married to Gauri, and not Kajol. To which the reply was *toh kya hota hai*. So, do you understand what I'm saying? They see them as if they actually belong together.

Nirmal: *You come from a literary family with your father as one of the best in Urdu lyrics. What according to you is the status of Urdu in our films? Do you think Urdu will ever be revived in Bollywood films?*

Zoya: Farhan speaks Urdu and much better than I do. See, you can't use a language that is not going to be understood, though I think the audience loves the sound of Urdu. It depends on the film. Then again the songs and melodies are changing—where do you put it in? Every film wants an item song. The songs that you're listening to are the ones that are being pumped—that's not the entire album. Urdu is still there in the lyrics. But those songs are not being pushed or marketed. If you hear the whole album, you'll be surprised.

Also, I think the language in the film and the dialogue depends on the subject. I don't think everybody uses it, and I don't think everybody can use it. You can't make a film like *Satya* and have Urdu. It depends on how you are using it. Naseer speaks Urdu in *Zindagi...* and Farhan writes Urdu poetry.

Nirmal: *What about adaptation from literature? Is it easy to do so? Don't you feel you have a responsibility towards Urdu language and literature to keep it alive, especially since you come from a great literary background?*

Zoya: Well, people do make adaptations. *Parineeta* is one example. People have to stop adapting *Devdas*. Vishal Bhardwaj has done an adaptation of Shakespeare. He's done other adaptations as well—such as *Omkara, Maqbool, The Blue Umbrella*.

I haven't done it yet, so I can't say. But of course it could be done. I would like to do it once, and it would be a great exercise also. Yes, it makes sense that someone like me should attempt to carry on the tradition of the language because I can.

Preeti: *How does a director depict a character that is distanced from her in terms of social milieu, landscape and psyche? For example, for a person with a privileged background to make a movie like* Peepli Live *— what does it require?*

Or for that matter, for you to imagine the psyche of not one but three different men in ZNMD, how do you do it?

Zoya: Well, it takes a lot of research—reading articles, books on the subject, maybe even visiting a particular region, seeing movies, etc. And of course, making up—after all, it is fiction.

I feel men are easier to depict than women. Women are way more complicated, more unpredictable and more layered. I find it more difficult to write women. I'm not saying women are better; all I'm saying is that they are more complicated. Also, men don't have hormones that go up and down. Why does every man say, 'I don't understand women!' Every woman says, 'You know how men are!'

Nirmal: *Is it possible for you to go back to making a small-budget film after making one like ZNMD?*

Zoya: Of course. I'm sure.

Preeti: *Can you imagine making a 10-million film?*

Zoya: Right now? The way things are—so expensive—I don't think anyone can imagine making a 10-million film. It is very tough. Like, maybe Anurag Kashyap would have spent that much or a little more on *The Girl in Yellow Boots*, but he shot it for 13 days and everybody worked for free. But I don't know. I don't decide on the budget before I write a story.

Preeti: *What about pressure and expectations from within the industry that after making a big-budget movie, why did you make a small film?*

Zoya: That doesn't bother me. I don't even think about that. I mean in terms of expectation or in terms of pressure, what I do feel is from the feedback I got from people who watched *ZNMD*, from the audience and people who wrote to me on Facebook—my inbox was flooded. It moved them. They felt something. They didn't just get entertained and had a laugh, but it also moved them. They felt one with a certain philosophy in the film. To me that is pressure. Anybody who felt a particular way about my film, be it *Luck by Chance*, or is going to watch a film of mine should come back with something. They should feel something. Whether the budget is bigger, whether my star is bigger... that doesn't bother me.

Nirmal: *Do you think it's easier to make a realistic film like* Gangs of Wasseypur *where you recreate a rural scene and a stock plot, a couple of abuses, costumes, actors from National School of Drama (NSD), whereas in a film like ZNMD you have to create an entire story as well as characters from scratch, a make-believe story?*

Zoya: It is difficult to make any movie. There is a great quote of Akira Kurosawa which says that whether it's a good film or a bad film, you wake up very early in the morning. Every film has got its own set of complexes. It is hugely difficult to make a film. It is a huge exercise. *Gangs of Wasseypur* must have been a tough film to make.

Preeti: *Talking of expectations, why is it that directors who have made brilliant first films then sometimes make films without much of a story – it's like conning the audience.*

Zoya: The trouble maybe starts when you begin to think what the audience will like as opposed to what you like. What would I like this character to do now? They are very worried about—this won't work or that won't. Nobody knows what the audience is going to like.

Courtesy: Shonali Bose.

Indie filmmaker Shonali Bose spent the better part of her childhood in Calcutta and Mumbai. She then moved to Delhi and studied at Miranda House, Delhi University, where she completed her Bachelor of Arts degree. She earned her Master's degree in political science from Columbia University, New York. Fate had other plans for this devoted student of history. The academically inclined Bose casually dipped her fingers into cinema at the University of California, Los Angeles (UCLA) Film School without realizing that filmmaking would swallow her whole.

Shonali Bose met her husband, Bedabrata Pain, at Columbia, where they were both heavily involved in activism. A research scientist at NASA for a good 15 years, Pain then entered filmmaking with his directorial debut, *Chittagong* (2012), co-written with Bose. She had her two sons while she pursued her Master of Fine Arts (MFA) in Directing at UCLA. They lost their elder son in an unfortunate electrical accident in 2010.

Bose's first feature film, *Amu*, was released in 2005. A young Indian–American, Kajori Roy aka Kaju (Konkona Sen Sharma), makes the classic *back to your roots* journey to India, but uncovers much more than she had bargained for. Along with Kabir (Ankur Khanna), her newfound friend, the adopted Kaju unveils a tragic truth that ties up her obscure origins with the 1984 Sikh genocide in Delhi.

Amu was screened at the Berlin Film Festival and the Toronto Film Festival in 2005. The film received critical acclaim in India, the United States and Canada. *Amu* won the National Film Award for the Best Feature Film in English, 2005. But the success that Bose garnered for her debut film arrived after many hurdles. An Indian production house that had promised to finance the film backed out unexpectedly. Bose then approached American production companies who insisted on having an American as the main protagonist, but the filmmaker refused to compromise. Finally, she raised the money herself with the help of her husband.

The next uphill battle was against the Indian Censor Board. It accorded *Amu* an 'A' certificate because of the controversial content of the film. The film clearly awards responsibility to the Indian state for the horrific violence organized against the Sikh community in 1984, to which the censor board replied—'Why should young people know a history which is best buried and forgotten?' Bose made it her business to make sure that young people did not forget this act of state-sponsored terrorism.

After *Amu*, the next film that engaged Shonali Bose was *Chittagong*. She co-wrote and co-produced it with her husband who was the film's director. Here too, the activist-filmmaker duo reconstructed a neglected piece of Indian history set in erstwhile Bangladesh, a victorious armed rebellion engineered by school children and their teacher with the help of revolutionaries against the British Empire.

For this self-professed activist, the personal is political. Bose's film graph reflects this potent resolve in the subjects that she has chosen to tackle and her treatment of them. Her films stem from real-life experiences. Bose had been actively engaged with the survivors of the Delhi riots at relief camps, and still recalls the *siapa* (ceremonial wailing) that rang through the air. But the haunting trauma of the victims of the 1984 massacres in *Amu* is not merely a representation of suppressed historical facts, but also points to the pressing need to seek justice and rehabilitation for all those left behind. Bose and her husband have been incessantly vocal about the Sikh cause since their time at Columbia.

Running through Bose's films is also an attempt at decoding the personal loss of a loved one. Her work carries shades of her life. The mother–daughter relationship in *Amu* echoes the deep bond that she shared with her mother, and the pain of losing her. Similarly, the poignant portrayal of a young girl suffering from cerebral palsy in *Margarita, With a Straw* is inspired by Bose's own cousin, Malini, and, here too, the mother plays a pivotal role in the protagonist's (Laila) life.

'She is a brilliant mind trapped in a disobedient body' is how Shonali describes her central character, Laila, in *Margarita, With a Straw*. The same could be said for Bose. She makes courageous films in a disorderly world, where the depiction of unnerving truths is a thankless task. Bose's writing and filmmaking come from a truly personal space, but ring true because it is relevant to our times and our lives.

Loss and Survival—
The Cinema of Meaning

Nirmal: *Let's start with your childhood. How was it?*

Shonali: I grew up in Calcutta till I was 14 and then we moved to Bombay. Thereafter, I came to Delhi University and stayed in a hostel. But my entire upbringing had nothing to do with films at all; in fact, I grew up in a very sociopolitically charged atmosphere of activism, and I think my cinema reflects that. I grew up with a very deep sense of wanting to fight for social justice in the country and to do something in that direction. In fact, I would have gone into law or something similar, but then as I studied I realized that the system is so corrupt that I felt it would be frustrating to be within the legal system. So I remained an activist, continued as an activist and I just felt that I would be interested in awakening people's consciousness through a mass medium. For instance, a subject like *Amu* — the idea was to make it for an audience who doesn't know or care about this issue. So therefore, it's not a documentary film. It was made as a fictional narrative that will draw in people from different walks of life. That's the kind of cinema I'm interested in. I was also very involved in theatre, though as an actor, not as a director.

Preeti: *Tell us a little about your parents and the kind of family life you had. Were you part of a joint family or was it a nuclear set up?*

Shonali: My parents are Bengalis, and I grew up in Calcutta with my grandparents living with us. I have one younger sister. My father and mother got separated when I was around eight. We continued to live with my paternal grandparents. They stood by my mother and did not want their grandchildren to be uprooted. My father left the house, got married again, but he also lived in Calcutta with his wife. We (my sister and I) would spend time with him over the weekends, and we were with our grandparents and our mother from when I was about eight years old.

One of my relatives was born with cerebral palsy — the umbilical cord strangulated her during birth, which stopped oxygen from going to her brain, and her motor skills got affected. Emotionally and intellectually you're absolutely fine, not mentally retarded. In those day it was called spastic, but the technical term is cerebral palsy. Today they say differently abled. It's politically incorrect to say spastic. But at that time, they didn't have that awareness. There was nothing in India, and so my aunt went abroad to study and then came back and set up the first institution in Bombay, called the Spastic Society of India. And my mother set it up in Calcutta with a friend of hers who also had a child with the same complication, except he also had mental retardation. So my mother remained in that sector working with handicapped children.

My father used to work as an engineer, but quite early in his life he left his profession and became a *sanyasi*. Finally, after my mother's death he moved towards spirituality, and he was the person who really exposed me to poverty because he would go and feed the poor ... it must have been connected with something religious. Even earlier, we had always been conscious of whoever worked in our house; we would go and stay in their houses. He imbued in me that sense of really caring about those who're not as well off. I feel that my parents awakened compassion in me. Interestingly, they're not political people. In fact, when I was associated with the Students Federation of India (SFI) during my time in Miranda House, my mother would get apprehensive. Their compassion did not come from an intellectual plane, but from their hearts.

My maternal aunt, Brinda Karat (renowned political activist), lived with us when I was very young. She was a formative influence in my life. She lived with us till she got married, for about five to six years. It was also the time when they had to go underground. Now she was in Communist Party of India (Marxist) [CPI(M)], so she imbued in me, right from an early age, a love for communism because my generation and certainly the generation afterwards, after the fall of the Soviet Union, had an attitudinal shift that communism is not the cool thing anymore. But before that, generally Indians moved towards the progressive Left perspective, but that kind of changed from my generation. Since my mentoring was from a family member, I grew up with a strong grounding in communism. So from an early age, I was studying Marxism and really appreciating it.

Preeti: *Considering that Brinda Karat was politically so active, did your parents somewhere also try to shield you fearing that you might end up being an activist yourself?*

Shonali: No, not as a child. I was in lots of rallies and nobody was like 'no don't take her'. There was no such thing in the family. But when I was in college, for instance, I remember this distinctly because I was in the SFI and my mother was like 'no, focus on studies' because I was also the Debating and Dramatic Society President in the first year itself, and so that's how she was. My mother was from Miranda House, and so was my aunt, Brinda. So for her it was like continuing a tradition. She wanted me to continue the tradition of being a theatre artiste. In fact, Amitabh Bachchan was in Kirori Mal College, and he was used to act with her as a lead actor. Also, I was shining in academics; I topped Delhi University in History. At that time, she warned me against standing for elections. But it was never a fight. It was her opinion, which I totally disregarded. She died when I was in the final year of college. I was only 21, so I was too young to know how she would have reacted to anything further.

Nirmal: *Were films a big part of your family?*

Shonali: Very little. Television only came into our lives when I was 13. There were no DVDs. So anytime there was something in the theatre, we would lap it up—like I remember *Pather Panchali* and how it impacted me. In the time that we grew up in, we didn't have access to films at home. We weren't well off enough. Television came really late into our family and then you're just restricted to what is being shown there. I remember *The Sound of Music* and *Pather Panchali* really clearly because I loved them both. I was in Loreto House, and we were taken by the school also to see films. But I can't say that films were a major influence in my growing up at all, and there was no question that I would have anything to do with films. I loved acting and that came naturally because my mother was an actor. She was doing *Sakharam Binder* at that time. She was doing both Hindi and English theatre, and she was the lead. I grew up in rehearsals and on stage, and in college that's what I pursued. That was my passion; I wanted to be an actor. Not professionally, but as a passion I love acting and being on stage—it has nothing to do with films.

Nirmal: *Do you think that films like* Pather Panchali *in the early stages of your life affected your filmmaking later?*

Shonali: *Pather Panchali*—100%. We actually studied it; it was our text. We actually read the original in Bengali. If I think back later, my own taste of cinema has been neo-realism and I just can't break away from that. I'm not interested in the fantastical. *Pather Panchali* stands out in my memory, not only affecting me as a person because it made me weep and made me feel for the plight of India and the lives of all these people—it affected me emotionally—but it also stands out for me as a filmmaker because it really inspired me.

Also, that film, within this repertoire of films, stands out because I watched the rest of the trilogy when I was studying film, and not as a child.

Nirmal: *At what point of time did you decide to make a film for yourself?*

Shonali: So, I was doing History Honours. It was my passion to teach History. That's what I wanted to do in my life. When I joined Delhi University for pursuing History Honours, people like Uma Chakravarti, the HOD, and Prem Chaudhary awakened my passion for History and modern India. History helped me to connect the dots. Sumit Sarkar's book just stands out in my memory for forming me as a person for the kind of understanding it conveyed. In school, you're just studying crap. You're just revering Gandhi and all that, and then I just remember the excitement of reading about the compromises made by Gandhi, etc.—to just look at all History in that way was very exciting for me. It just changed me.

I would have gone to Jawaharlal Nehru University (JNU) and continued studying History, but due to the tragedy of my mother dying in the prime of her life only at

42 years of age, I could not continue. She was in Bombay, and went to Nanavati Hospital with some minor ailment and the doctor basically perforated her intestines with his 10 fingers, which ultimately led to two months in coma and then death. She went in with a minor ailment—she was just feeling sick and throwing up, she had some stomach infection, and the doctor opened up to see and in doing that he killed her. I just had such an intense anger that I couldn't be in India, so I had to leave.

I would never have gone abroad otherwise because I didn't have that interest, even though with my generation the excitement to study abroad was very high. I just needed to leave India, so I left. I didn't get funding for History, I got it for Political Science at Columbia. At that point the idea was that I just needed to leave and go away—the pain was too enormous for me to stay on. So, there I was at Columbia University, in the Department of Political Science, one of the top departments in the country, and I hated it. It was so conservative.

I remember I had done a paper on Naxalbari and the Telangana, and I wrote the paper as an activist, out of a passion, though it was extremely academic—I was trained in that, I had topped Delhi University. But it was written with passion because I can't be removed from the history of my people, which is also such recent history. Even when I was making the presentation, it was not as if it was something far away from me. I cared about what happened. So that was not Columbia University's thing at that time. You know that would probably be more new school for social research, which just was starting out in New York. I felt Columbia was just sucking the life out of me, and I had full funding for a seven-year Ph.D. I quit after my Master's. I realized this was not for me.

At the same time an other aunt, Radhika Roy, and her husband, Prannoy Roy, came to New York. She was at *India Today* and her husband was at the Delhi School of Economics. She came to do a six-week course at New York University in television and video. They had no background in television and video, and they stayed with me in my dorm (which just makes me laugh today) where they had to use a shared loo. While she was doing this course, I was the actor in her exercises. I could act really well and it was convenient for her. I was on the other side of the camera and I felt, *bhai yeh to bada acha hai*. So I thought I'll also try to do this—this seems very interesting. Then it took me a year to save up the money to do it, during which I was doing odd jobs like babysitting, etc. You're allowed to work in the US after your degree. I had finished my Master's, and technically I was allowed to stay for one more year in the country and work.

I got a job at Manhattan Cable Television. There once a week, you got to direct, edit and produce a 10-minute piece on some contemporary issue. I chose police brutality and issues that just really excited me, and I realized what I could do with images to affect people, and again the battles happened because people were conservative. What drew me was not acceptable, and I just remember those battles of how I wanted to portray politics and how they would not let me. So I did the six-week course. When I finished the course, which was the following summer of 1988 in New York, I was sure this is what I wanted to do. I applied to New York University, University of Southern California, UCLA, all these film schools and again it was just fate because I had no money, and if I hadn't got a scholarship, I wouldn't have done it and would have come back to India. Just as my visa expired and I was to come back to India, I got a full scholarship at UCLA Film School, which is one of the top film schools in the country. So I joined UCLA. Even at that time, I thought that I'd rather just be an activist full time because by then I was very active with the Indian

Progressive Study Group, an organization in New York. In fact, Siddharth Varadarajan, who is now the editor of *The Hindu*, was an activist there at the same time. At that point, I thought I would do one semester. What I'm trying to say is that I was not passionate about films, but had got full funding to go to UCLA. It was a five-year programme then (MFA in Directing), but now it's a four-year one. I almost declined it considering that I was really excited about being a full-time activist. My husband asked me to try one semester saying that I could always quit if I hated it.

Preeti: *Were you married by then?*

Shonali: Yes, I joined UCLA in 1992, and I got married in 1990. Bedo was at Columbia University and also an activist. We were at some demonstration about the Indian Peace Keeping Force in Sri Lanka and that's how we met.

So then I made my first short film—a two-minute film in October. We joined UCLA in September. That's when I knew that this is what I have been made for; this is my passion—to direct cinema. I just loved doing it. I loved conceptualizing something that I wanted to convey and the creative process of doing that and then seeing its impact. Within one month of Film School, there was no looking back. I knew that I had found my calling. At that point, I was 29 years old. That was how I got into cinema.

Many years later, at one of the *Amu* screenings when I told the History Department of a college that it was my dream that I would be teaching History, they said I was already teaching history through my cinema, so it's good that whatever happened changed my path.

Nirmal: *You never got back to acting.*

Shonali: No, I stopped acting because today there are so many roles for South Asians, all of them such amazing and wonderful opportunities. In my time you would get stereotypical Indian roles, which I would rather die than do.

Nirmal: *You never acted in your own film. Weren't you tempted to go in front of the camera?*

Shonali: No (laughs).

I wouldn't do it in my own first film. Actually, I have a momentary role in *Chittagong*. I would rather be directed by other people than as a director focusing on directing myself.

Nirmal: *Listening to you, it is evident that you come from an activist, left-of-the-centre, extreme communism – did it affect your filmmaking and its thought process? You come from an activist family – nobody was really doing a nine-to-five job, going back home then watching a movie and sleeping at 10 in the night; not that kind of life. Did that affect your persona and also your filmmaking?*

Shonali: Only my aunt, Brinda. It would not be true to say that the rest are. My parents were involved in the social sector – a social consciousness – the NGO sector where you do things like the disability movement. We are all extremely secular.

But I am hard-core Left of the Left of the Left. I am not ashamed of it and I'm not hiding that. CPI(M) for me was very conservative and that emerged at Columbia University and definitely in Miranda House also where I found that I wasn't interested in the Left party coming to power because then it's the same about just being in power. It is about the empowerment of people. We're still stuck with this problem of how people in this country are to be empowered. Just last night, I was watching my student's thesis film, *Lifting the Veil*, and politics was there. It was a documentary.

Courtesy: Shonali Bose.

Nirmal: *Now I see that a lot of your experiences are reflected in the film. In* Amu, *the mother's side is very strong – the mother–brother relationship, the* nani's *relationship. Also, the choice of picking up a girl, the boy dies but the girl survives. Is it deliberate on your part? Do you see yourself in the little girl who survived?*

Shonali: Well, I didn't really plan…

First and foremost, I'm drawn to writing women characters. I come from a women-oriented family; women are very important in my life. Maybe being a woman myself, it comes naturally. Even in *Margarita, With a Straw*, interestingly, it's a mother–daughter relationship that I highlight. I guess that's what moves me. My mother dying and then my *mausi* stepping in as my mother. It's a core formative thing for me as a person—it draws me all the time to dealing with that relationship. In both films, the mother-daughter relationship is the primary relationship being dealt with.

Nirmal: *How old were you at the time of your mother's death? That impacted you a lot.*

Shonali: I was 21 years in the final year of college. It was a watershed event; as I said, I had to leave the country and, as a result, it changed the course of what would happen to me in life. I was totally set for Ph.D. in History and excited to study in JNU, and stay on as a teacher.

Nirmal: *All this must have impacted you greatly. When one looks back at the film, it seems that you wanted to avoid facing that (mother's death) because when the mother dies there is just a little bit of Brinda Karat crying, and you somehow pan the camera—I noticed that you did not dwell much on it. Probably you could have highlighted that particular incident a little more when the little girl loses her mother. The little girl is not with her mother but hiding somewhere else, and Brinda Karat goes on looking for her. Was that you? Were you aware of such a statement made through the film?*

Shonali: No. I wrote the flashback sequence just once, by hand when I had just decided to write *Amu*. I was anxious since this was my first feature. As a filmmaker, the best way is to be as personal as possible and as honest, and go to your place of pain if possible—if you can, open up your place of pain and write, and you'll make an honest film that will touch people. I realized that I had to deal with motherhood and that was coming to my huge second watershed, which was the death of my son. I left India because I'd lost my mother, and I came back from the US because of the death of my son just after *Chittagong*. My life's been like that. With his death, I realized how I hadn't managed to deal with my mother's death at all. When I went away to the US, my whole family was there together, but I was all alone in America dealing with the death of the person who was the centre of my life. My father had left us, I mean he's amazing and I love him, but the core relationship was my mother because she was such an amazing person. She was so cool, just fantastic, loving, the perfect mother. There wasn't even an age gap because when I kissed my first boyfriend I could tell her. To then lose that person at 21.... I remember in Delhi University, I got molested. Some guy grabbed my breast, and my mother was there at that time (I remember this because it was just before her death) and how strong she was. Just standing up and fighting for your rights because the principal at that time said that we had called it upon ourselves. We did not even have any eve-teasing cells. We went on a whole campus-wide action and only St. Stephens didn't join in. We went up to the VC's office and I was speaking there because then I found out that it happened to many girls, that humiliation, but they were just too scared to say anything. It happened to me and I immediately went on stage, I shouted and said, '*In gundo ko nikalo*'. They made me go to the police station, and I told them, 'I have handed the *gunda* to you, why are you making me identify him again?' I was not scared to speak. In fact, I was in a *saree*, ironically, but it turned out to be a backlash against me—'You are a bold woman, and so you are inviting it on yourself'. The principal, T.S. Rukmani, gave me a bad character certificate saying that I had brought shame to the college because it came in the papers and we had made a huge scene about it. I said, 'You should feel proud that (we *gheraoed* her, we were not scared) we made a huge scene'. I went home and cried because it felt horrible to be touched like that and it felt horrible to be told that I had brought this on myself; that I was responsible for being touched like that. At all levels, my mother was just such a strong person and amazing in her support. Soon after that she died.

In America, if anyone even said the word mother, I could not handle it—it was like a place of pain. So I thought—I have to write about motherhood. Can I do that? It would just make me weep. My mother died in 1986 and I started writing in 2002. That's a long time to not have dealt with the pain. I didn't have the ability to deal with the pain. Maybe *Amu* was therapeutic for me unconsciously. I would never think that the *Amu* flashback scene is actually about me. I always thought that I was writing a mother-daughter relationship—Keya and Kaju—their deep loving relationship. And to have the courage to write that is difficult enough because I'm going back to memories to write about that relationship. So in that first writing by hand that I did in my notebook, I described that scene. The train comes in between, she's calling out to Shanno and Shanno can't hear her, and that never got changed—never got changed. I wrote about 20 drafts, but that sequence always remained pure. So maybe that is something—of course, it has nothing to do with anything that happened in my life—but in a way, your mother leaves—and that is symbolic. I haven't analysed it.

Preeti: *It was a brilliant scene.*

Shonali: It just came to and I had to write it like that. So I wasn't conscious as a filmmaker—I didn't even think of it. In fact many years later, I was seeing a therapist and he said, 'It is so clear who you are in *Amu*.' I asked him whether I was Kaju or maybe Keya, but he said that I was the little girl, and I said, 'No way'!

Nirmal: You were definitely the little girl, but you were also Kaju. The way you have contextualized her character in the film is such that she represents you. The way she dresses, the way she speaks is just like you. I can see your body language, the way you speak, is reflected in Kaju – Konkana was almost like you. Including your real mausi in the film as well as your own Leftist proclivities are evident. Without shouting about it being a woman's film, it was a very strong film.

Preeti: One had read the background of the film, about the carnage, but when I was watching it, half an hour into the movie (typically these sort of movies turn out to be very propagandist) I thought to myself – when are we reaching that point? Kaju is exploring the town but she is not talking about the riots. I am wondering – when will she talk about the riots? You've been very successful in being able to build it up, and weaving the personal and the political. It doesn't come across as propaganda. Even in terms of the aesthetics of the movie, you really get drawn into the narrative of Kaju and then you relate to the character. If from the very beginning it had been about state-sponsored genocide then you would probably only watch it as a documentary.

Shonali: Completely. That was a very conscious choice that I made thinking that an audience is an audience. It doesn't know or care about this issue, and how do I draw people in when it is neither a Sikh audience nor an activist audience. I am not trying to reach those people. They are going to watch the film anyway. I am trying to reach an audience that does not care about politics, and how am I to make them care about this genocide that everybody has been made to think of as a communal riot caused by Hindus? How am I to change them to think of something they don't even think of in these terms, that is, state-sponsored terrorism? Such a phrase is unnatural for people and they won't accept it.

It was a challenge for me to be completely opposite of an activist, completely put that side away because I was an activist in the camps. I worked in the camps. As soon as the three days ended, the History department formed a relief committee, and we went into Trilokpuri and other riot-inflicted areas. That experience is very strong in my memory but I thought that I wouldn't write the film as an activist. I would bring in the relief camp scene, but I was not going to write this entire film from a place of anger. And that was a decision I had to actively make because it would have been very easy to write a tom-tomming film. The anger was still there that nobody had been served justice. 1984 happened and soon after I lost my mother. At the time 1984 happened, I had not lost anybody close in my life. So I didn't know how to deal with death. I was just 18, going into the camps, and these women were just holding me and weeping and doing *siapa*. And I didn't know what to say to a person who's just lost his/her son, father or husband.

So I made this film, never having dealt with pain and right after that I lost my mother. Then I had never seen a person on fire. I made *Amu* without ever seeing a human being on fire. But that's how my son died. He went on fire. It is funny that I made a film in which I comforted women, who watched their sons on fire. Imagine seeing your child on fire. What a terrible thing. I could not imagine such a horrifying thing. So I had made a film in which I thought I wouldn't show many people, but just the impact felt when a little girl had to see her father on fire. Imagine when 20 years later, I had to see my 16-year-old son on fire because his shaver malfunctioned and he came out screaming from the bathroom. It was exactly like *Amu*. I couldn't put the fire out, and he was in the hospital and he died.

I had to leave America because I couldn't stay there, and I came back to India. So my journey as a filmmaker and my own life's tragedies have been very tied up in that sense.

In *Chittagong*, the small role I was talking about is the turning point in the film when the boy—Jhunku—sees another teenager being shot by the British police and that makes him join politics. We couldn't find an actor good enough to just run to the boy's dead body, and react to it right there and then because it was such a small role. So who would play that role? I said that I would play it. It was February 2010, and I was getting make up done and being dressed to do that role. I just thought that if I imagined Ishan's death—I couldn't even think that—I wouldn't be able to act because that would just make me go to pieces. So I decided that it was my mother's body and that I would react to my mother's dead body, and that's how I would do the role. So then in *Chittagong*, I did the role of a mother whose 16-year-old son had died. So in a way, both *Amu* and *Chittagong* are about Ishan's death.

Then I started writing *Margarita, With a Straw* on what would have been his 17th birthday. He died in September 2010, and in January he would have turned 17. So on the day after his birthday, I celebrated his 17th birthday. I was happy all day and I was happy for the amazing life that he had lived and how proud I was to be his mother. That is what I celebrated. The next day I just sat down and wrote *Margarita, With a Straw*. It is about a person who has cerebral palsy, but it's actually her journey of self-acceptance. It is about doing the inner work so as to withstand all the storms that life may put forward before you. It could be disability or death—all kinds of things. But to have a strong core, as a human being you need to do the inner work and connect with yourself because most of the time we are in denial of our pain. We fill our lives with the Internet,

A still from *Margarita, With a Straw*.
Courtesy: Shonali Bose.

relationships, drinking and other things to fill the pain, but we don't really go to our place of pain. *Margarita, With a Straw* is that journey. It's the point of view of a person with a disability, but that is not what's important; anybody can through that journey. Ishan's death made me write it in that way. She, in fact, loses her mother in the film. I guess it's because I am drawn to dealing with death. So, all the three films are really in a way to do with my life.

Preeti: *Do you think there is a difference in the way you dealt with your mother's death and Ishan's death? How have you dealt with so much pain, and still managed to do so much work, and stay in a constructive and positive frame of mind? You have clearly not become bitter or disillusioned.*

Shonali: When Ishan died, I felt that I had to really deal with the pain. I was unable to do so with my mother's death because I just could not let it slip by. I felt had to sit with the pain and hold it. I didn't actually understand that it was the process of letting go. I had not studied Buddhist texts as I was a hard-core atheist. All I knew was that I would not ignore the pain. I would not pretend that my life was fine and be strong. I would sit with my pain and embrace it by myself. I would not make the mistake of avoiding this pain with Ishan. I could not have on with this feeling of being wounded as I did with my mother's death.

At the moment when I was emptying my mother's ashes in to the ocean, I saw her, and two years later my sister said that she saw the same thing (my sister and I saw her in the same *saree* with her arms outstretched). I felt filled with light and I was laughing, wondering why everyone in the boat was crying. I was comforting my *mausis* and my father, and I felt like I could support the world. I felt so strong. It was like a spiritual energy that came into me at that moment of death. After that I went to America, met my husband who was a hard-core Marxist, and he made me say that it was just my imagination. So I turned my back on that spiritual experience.

With Ishan's death, I remember that at the funeral I spoke from a place of light and strength. I wasn't faking it. I woke up on the day of his funeral, wore a red *saree* and wrote on my Facebook page, 'Please come for my son's funeral in red to celebrate his life, not to mourn his death'. So the whole school was there on that day, the teachers and the parents, all howling because they didn't know how to handle it. There I was, the mother who showed them the way. But that just came organically; I was not trying to be strong… you cannot be. As I told you, when I was practising for the role in *Chittagong*, my body went to pieces and my insides were shaking. I couldn't even imagine one of my children dying but then when it happened, something filled me. I looked at his photograph, his smiling face, which gives me so much joy and energy every time I look at it—as I looked at it, my body got filled with light and energy. I just stood up and spoke in a vibrant red *saree*, and I said—'This is the insight that came to me—that in life you think that somebody has to be there till their late nineties and only then it's okay for them to die, even then you feel sad when your grandparents die'. But it's not about measuring of the length of the journey, it is about the quality of the journey. Doesn't matter how long he lived on this earth, but Ishan had an amazing journey. He didn't have to be here longer. So we shouldn't be sad about it. For him, he's part of the universe now. He had 16 beautiful years that we got to share with him. That changed everybody in that hall. There were about 500 people and they came out feeling light because I, as the mother, felt like that. After that it's a hard battle to keep that, but I just organically felt like that on the day of the funeral. Our notion is that somebody has to be old, but it's not like that. I didn't look at it as a tragedy. You are born and you're going to die, and it doesn't mean that you have to die when you're old and if you die young then it's a tragedy.

After that, for that one year, I couldn't come back because I needed to get the visa. For one year I was there with my younger son, Vivaan, in that house and lived with the pain. I learned to deal with the pain by myself, and also that I didn't have to seek other people to come and hug me. I was not afraid of it. I think that is a turning point in a person's life. With my mother's pain, I would want somebody to comfort me, hold me and be with me, and that's what made me rush into marriage. With Ishan's death, I took the pain and I said, 'Okay, I'm not scared of you'. So I'm going to cry now for a couple of hours, and that is okay and it's not the end of the world. I'll come out of it. I can't keep crying non-stop. I was not afraid of such a difficult pain, of remembering the burning—that's a very terrifying thing—to have nightmares. That's when I started seeing a therapist. I wanted to take all the necessary steps to deal with this. I was not going to avoid it. I would sit with the memories till they stopped scaring me and till I rose above it.

I have written this—that my son gave me the gift of his birth; he was my first-born and he changed me as a human being. He gifted me with his death because he helped me get in touch with myself, with my emotions and with a sense of peace. And till *Amu*, I felt that I was 44 and I hadn't made my next film. All these people who started after me like Anurag—in fact when I had done *Amu*, *Black Friday* was also releasing at that time, but it had not been able to come out, and he came and touched my feet—Dibakar and others had not even made films yet. I was like that I've only made *Amu* and I haven't been able to make any other film. I had two children and I had chosen being a mother as my first role, and thank. But I thank God that I made the decision not to be in that race. I wanted to be a full-time mother. I didn't put them in day care. It was a conscious decision that I didn't want my children in day care. So I, the feminist, was the housewife because I wanted to be at home with my children and something made me do that. Therefore, I couldn't be making a film every year. Thank God I didn't. But I used to feel terrible about it. I used to feel that I had been left behind despite being talented. Now people write books and articles, and I'm not even mentioned. *Amu* came out at a time when multiplexes weren't there. So it hardly had a release. We had some five prints. And people have made much worse cinema, and I used to just be caught in this terrible thing—that feeling of insecurity and envy—a feeling that I was talented and nobody was recognizing it. Ishan's death brought such a sense of peace, like who cares! Now when I make a film it's from that place of peace, while earlier I wanted the recognition. I would have always made my kind of cinema. But now I don't care about recognition or the race; all that is unimportant for me.

Jo ho, so ho. This understanding is not a fatalistic one; there is a difference, because I'm an activist and there are certain things that you fight. Globalization or injustice is not *jo ho, so ho.* I will be out there in the frontlines fighting it. But there are bigger things that you cannot control — you cannot control other human beings, and you cannot control illness or death. There have been deaths (not as close as mother or father) in the past two years since Ishan's and I feel the pain of other people, but I take it in a very philosophical way. That is the most important thing because we are most terrified of death — our own death and of those we love. That fear is gone from me. I had it after my mother's death for 20 years, but when my son died I lost that fear. It makes me appreciate life moment by moment, and I'm filled with a sense of beauty, awe and peace. That is the gift Ishan gave me and continues to give me.

Nirmal: *Were you at all daunted by the technicalities involved in making a film, for example, the cameras, lighting and other technologies?*

Shonali: At UCLA Film School, you are required to be a DP and shoot somebody else's film and then be a sound technician too. Our training forced us to fulfil every technical position. We actually loaded the films, acted as an assistant camera person or would be setting up the lights.

So that prepares you hugely. But what I was intimidated by was the fact that I was still coming out of film school (where I did all this very effectively with a crew of 10 people because we were making student films) and then I had children, and a four-year gap as a mother. Then suddenly, I started to making my first feature film. I had never been on a feature film set. I had only done student films. I was like *itne saare trucks meri film ke liye*. I was used to a 10-people crew; technology does not intimidate me because I don't really care nor does it impact creative decisions because I know exactly what I want and that is great. I knew this when I was standing there that I had the confidence and I knew where the cameras should be. And also because the script was written in such detail by me and imagined by me. But before that I was a bit nervous, thinking to myself, *will I know*? The crew certainly felt that I did not know. For one, I had come from America, it was my first feature film and everybody had more experience than me. They had done three to four feature films. Plus, I was a woman. But very early on they saw that I was extremely clear about what I wanted and I was not bothered by ego. So for me as a director, I firmly believe that you are with the actor and that I would not be bothered by technology.

The drama is about performance. They were trying to intimidate me. I didn't know how to shoot a moving car scene. As if we had that luxury in school films! But these men feel that they have to show off this knowledge and I could see that sneering a little bit.... I was like I don't care where you put the camera or how you mount it, that is your job. This is what I want—I want these two people who are crying in the car, and I want a tight shot and I don't know this word that you are saying (I still can't remember it).

I was really without ego when I made *Amu*. For instance, the DP and the art director had a huge fight. One said, 'I won't dress the set', the other said, 'I won't light it...' till she says sorry, till he says sorry. So I went to both of them and touched their feet and I said, 'Without you, the film is finished.' I told them that I couldn't do the film without them. So I said sorry on behalf of that person. And they were really embarrassed because people have huge egos, and this is what I discovered, and I had zero ego.

I am a technophobe. Actually, I have taught technical classes at New York Film Academy and when you are teaching you have to know, but my brain does not store technical terms. I can somehow manage to put my own DVD on. So when I have to teach, I read and remember but after such a long gap, I cannot recall. Nor do I care about it. What I care about is about getting the performance I want and getting the shots I want. For instance, I do have a strong perspective on where I want my camera, but ultimately it's all about the actor. Most directors, sad to say, ignore their actors and for them it's all about the camera.

Nirmal: *Did the technical team try to scare you by asking questions such as which camera is to be used, which filter is to be used, etc.?*

Shonali: No, there is no such thing. I have never heard of such a thing. It's not like that. No DP would ever do that. That is a DP's job. DP is not meant to ask *ki kya filter lagaye*. I have never heard such a thing. It sounds very backward. My DP had an outlook like mine, and we spent a lot of time looking at artists such as Renoir. I still have those books that I had given to him for reference for *Amu*. The paintings reflected the kind of feel I wanted for my films. We spent weeks and weeks in Los Angeles on what should be the feel that we wanted for the film. No DP, who's a good DP, will ask the director whether I use Hydrargyrum medium-arc iodide (HMI) here or do I use a filter. That is shocking to me.

Preeti: *You spoke about the importance of the relationship between the director and the actors. So tell us in detail about the* casting. *How did you visualize the characters in* Amu? *Why did you zero in on the actors that you finally picked?*

Shonali: I saw 100 girls for Kaju in the US because I felt it had to be an Indian–American. I didn't feel an Indian actor could pull it off. And I had gone to Calcutta to meet Aparna Sen for playing Keya, the mother's role, and Konkona was wandering in the background. I would call her Aparna *mausi* and I knew her very well. I also knew her elder daughter, Dona, from her previous marriage, as we had grown up together. I didn't know Konkona. Aparna said that she was directing her next film and wouldn't be able to do it. She had read the script by then and she asked me whom I had thought of for the role of Kaju. I told her that I was casting abroad for that character. Then she suggested Konkona and said that her younger daughter was very good. In my head I was like *yeh kya museebat hai*. I have come to take the mother and she's pushing her daughter — this is super embarrassing!

So I went back to America and continued auditioning girls. I had gone to meet Aparna in the summer because I could only work in my children's school vacation. That's the only way I made my cinema. They were off from July–August and December–January.

Preeti: *But then how long did you take to make the movie?*

Shonali: No, no, no. Shooting is different. But it takes a long time to prepare a movie. You have to put the crew and cast together. So I used to do that during my sons' vacations. They used to come with me to India and would be around me as I worked.

So I came back to India in December. *Mr. and Mrs. Iyer* was in the theatres. I went to PVR Saket, I watched it and I came out, and from the parking lot I called up Aparna *mausi* and said, 'Give the script to Konkona'. I was like she's playing a Tamilian so brilliantly — I mean I could not tell she's not a Tamilian! She read the script and called me back saying that she loved it. I asked her to come to Delhi for the audition and she was so desperate to do it. As soon as I saw her, I knew that she was my Kaju. But still I auditioned her and I didn't tell her. Then we thought and we were like yes. She got the National Award for *Mr. and Mrs. Iyer* and she was so excited. So that was Kaju.

With Keya, my own instinct was to go with an unknown person. I wanted Brinda to play the role even though she said she would spoil my film. My mother had told me that she was not the brilliant actor in the family, but Brinda. And my mother was a brilliant actor. She was in the *Far Pavilion* just before her death, and on stage she was astounding. My aunt had gone to study at Rada in England but then became a communist instead. She came back a communist instead of an actor. Brinda's exact words were — 'I will ruin your first film.' I think she had to take the party's permission, but she did it because of the subject matter. It was such a sensitive film and it dealt with a hard-core political issue. It was not that she was doing a frivolous film. As a matter of fact, everybody in the party just loved the film.

Nirmal: What was your relationship with the technicians? How did you develop a rapport with them? There are two kinds of directors — those who want to know everything and go trouble the technicians, and those who are not interested in how the trolley moves or how the lighting works as long as the work is done. Technicians are behind-the-scenes. How do you handle them?

Shonali: The thing is that 'HoDs' are the people a director deals with. You are not really dealing with the light guy who's holding the light. But I had a great relationship with every light guy and technician. I treated them as equals. On the sets of *Amu* I actually said that it was an equal set, and not a hierarchical one. Anyone can come to talk to me.

Otherwise, the director is protected and nobody has access to the director except the HoDs. Really young people just grew big on the sets of *Amu* because I saw their talent. So I saw the talent of someone like the production assistant, Sunil, and now he is about to direct his own film. He had become Rakesh Omprakash Mehra's and Aamir Khan's assistant. They were all juniors and couldn't have a conversation with me. The director was shielded; only HoDs could talk to her/him and I found it strange. The HoDs hated it if the director would interact with the junior technicians.

So there were two things I'd have to handle. One was how I would relate to the HoDs. With the HoDs, I had a fantastic relationship because of the script. This is what my experience through my three films has been. I'm a writer which many people may not be. Talented HoDs are just like 'Wow! What a script!' Immediately they have great respect for you because you wrote something that they are not seeing much in India. So they want to do the film and that's great. For example, Resul Pookutty who at that time hadn't got the Oscar yet, he is very intelligent and coming out of FTII, loved the script. He comes from an FTII background and we immediately clicked. He's got an Oscar, but still he'll do any of my films. *Margarita, With a Straw* is a small film, and he himself recorded the sound on the set. He had also done *Chittagong*. He values how we sync as directors. He and I, when we're talking about sound design, it's an exciting conversation. Now the technicalities he handles, he doesn't want me to say which mike is to be used. But when we're talking about having silence… first of all we are firm believers in sync sound; Resul and I believe that when you don't shoot sync it's an artificial performance because when you dub it, a discerning audience will catch it. Most Indian filmmakers will be like *yaar dub karade*, but I'll never compromise on that. So right away, Resul and I were in agreement on how to work. And this is one of the top sound technicians in the world and knows everything. I completely respect sound, and a film without good sound is not acceptable. I told everybody that Resul has the right to ask for perfect sound. We are not going to shoot till you quieten it down. When I made *Amu,* it was a rare thing to make a sync sound film in location. You make a sync sound film on set, but normally you don't do it in a location in Chandni Chowk. We were doing sync sound in crowded places. I gave him that respect because I myself believe in it. Then we both don't believe in just relying on music to create an emotion. We would think about the subconscious emotion we wanted to highlight and through what sound effect.

Then the art department. Now, I don't need to know the technicalities of how they make a set. They could see that I had a complete understanding of the authentic feel that I wanted to bring out—whether it's a working-class home or a middle-class one. So creatively, completely related to each other. Now as to how they would achieve that was their business, then they would show it to me and I would approve it. Nobody asked me 'how will I get the wall like that?' No technician speaks like that.

The DPs loved the script of the film as well. They didn't want me to tell them which angle to use, which camera, etc. Do I understand as a filmmaker what feel I want? Yes, I do. How do I want the scene to feel? But they don't need to be told how to achieve that feel. Even say music, Shankar-Ehsaan-Loy were so thrilled that we didn't go in and say *ki ek item number chahiye, ek emotional song,* etc. Everything I want is organic to my script. The technicians really respect that. They then deliver that technically. And I don't want them to replicate the work of other directors in my film, or I don't ask them to get the edginess of Anurag or something else of another director.

Nirmal: *Very few people have been both writer and director. You made the film and wrote the novel. How was that experience?*

Shonali: The book was written after the screenplay. Penguin came to me when I was editing and said that this was fantastic as a novel. I told them that I couldn't make it into a novel because I didn't have time. I could just write out my screenplay in words and that would have been crappy as a novel. I asked them to give me two years to write it as a whole novel, as a novel should be treated. I'm actually a good writer. But they wanted the book and the film to come out at the same time. I regret it actually because I'm embarrassed by the novel. So I wrote the book as I was editing the film.

Preeti: *What is your take on the whole debate of whether good literature can be transformed into good filmmaking?*

Shonali: I've in fact been offered a book and we are talking right now. I've been offered to make a film based on Chitra Banerjee Divakurni's latest novel. I read it and I was excited about it. So it is a challenge because I've always written my own screenplay. What will I use from the material/book and what will I bring to the material? There's no point if you're just directly doing it. You need to raise it to another level. What I will bring to the novel as the writer of the screenplay—that is how I am going to treat it when we get to that stage.

Writing my own screenplays and directing them is really easy because I've written it and have visualized it before I start directing it.

Nirmal: *At the time of making it did you ever find that you should have written it differently?*

Shonali: I don't believe in ever locking a thing in a way that is considered perfect and brilliant. I go into rehearsal.

I have my assistant there on the set and we rehearse. Now actors bring something to it and I'm always open as a director at every phase. The way actors say their dialogues or something similar completely changes us and I think 'Oh God! What was I thinking?' We note that down or record it. Then I go back that night and rewrite the scene completely. When I'm writing it, I'm attached to it. When I was working on *Margarita, With a Straw*, I was deeply attached to it and if you asked me to change something, I would say it was perfect. But in the next phase when my actors come in, I'm totally open and I'll rewrite anything. Then when I'm shooting at a location, there is a fresh perspective. Finally, when we're editing, we throw the script away. *Amu* is totally different if you read the novel. You can see the difference between the film and the book. The novel is based on the script that I went in with before editing. With the film, which is edited, you change structure, things which were very important had to get edited because it just didn't work.

Preeti: *How challenging is your role during the editorial process?*

Shonali: It is extremely painful. It's like a part of your body being cut. When she put the finished film together, it was three hours and I made it a one hour and forty-five minute film. I threw out an hour and twenty minutes of the film. If you haven't seen the deleted scenes, you must see them because they are wonderful. But in the structure, the scenes just slow the movie down. We needed it to be a tight film. So I am never self-indulgent.

Nirmal: *You are a Bengali, but you have made an authentically real film on Punjabis. Did you have a problem? Some of the scenes are so authentic. For example, one scene where the riot is about to start, Amu's mother is putting the food together and says 'Pehli roti kha ja'. I don't know whether you know this or not, but in*

Punjab great importance is attached to the 'pehli roti'. Punjabis are very superstitious about it. How did you pull it off?

Shonali: Actually, I am quarter Punjabi. My *nana* is Punjabi. In the Sehgal family, all of them are my aunts and uncles living in Delhi. There is a scene where Kaju is visiting Kabir's house. The family in the garden is actually my family, all my aunts and uncles, my mother's cousins. My *nana* is Punjabi and the other three grandparents are Bengali. But the thing is that I didn't grow up in Delhi and it's just the research that I always do. For example, in *Margarita, With a Straw*, there is a Maharashtrian mother. Even for that, I have done all my research. The authenticity comes from my research, and not because I have Punjabi genes. Anyway, the Westernized upper-class Punjabi is very different and you can't go by that. The thing is, for one, I have gone as an activist in many working-class Punjabi homes. Then I was also working a lot in relief camps and did follow up in their homes with Sikh families. So those memories have just stayed with me and I cannot forget certain details. I lived in the slums, because for me to be authentic, I needed to experience what they were doing. So that's just from my lived experience. I have actually lived with a lot of the Punjabi working-class families. I used to stay the night at their homes just so that I could understand their living conditions. This I am talking about 1997 when *Lifting the Veil* was made.

But I always research anything. Just because I am Bengali, I cannot miss my research even on that. My family is an upper-class, intellectual Bengali family of Calcutta, but that is not going to be like the Chitranjan Park middle-class family. I hung out a lot with the Chitranjan Park middle-class Bengalis. How they do up their house, how they interact, their milieu. That is not my family. My grandmother and others are all educated in England and are

English-speaking. For example, the Bengali *dida*, who is a typical Bengali grandmother, is not in the realm of my experience in my own family. But I researched all of that and spent a lot of time with middle-class Bengalis. So just because I am Bengali doesn't mean I can pull it off authentically, unless I am portraying my exact class background and my exact family.

Nirmal: *Being a student of History, you would have a keen sense of historical knowledge compared to other people. You were the 1984–1987 batch with the revised syllabus. So with you, the awareness is more. As a conscious student of History, did your subject shape your filmmaking, and in what way?*

Shonali: Definitely it shapes me as a person. I think, my continuing to be political is from the awareness... it's like *Alice in Wonderland,* just like going into a new, wonderful, amazing place to study social formations, modern India and people like Sumit Sarkar. It's just like you're looking at the world in a certain way and then click, you are looking at the world in another way. You look and you see that the past, present and future are so interconnected and continuous. As soon as you look at life like that, you are more equipped than others.

Preeti: *Why did you choose such a difficult subject for your comeback venture?*

Shonali: I don't shy away from subjects just because they are difficult or challenging. In fact, I find it challenging to find a way to tell a story that no one else is likely to tell and needs to be told. It takes me a long time to settle in on what film I want to make—because it takes so much out of me for a few years. It's like giving birth to a baby till he/she goes to preschool! It's intense.

Preeti: *The mother-daughter relationship is your forte. How is the treatment different in this film?*

Shonali: In a way it's very similar to *Amu*—in that they are extremely close and the centre of each other's world. The specificities are different. In *Amu*, the mother was from a Bengali family. She was a political activist and lived abroad. In *Margarita, With a Straw*, the mother is a simple Maharashtrian housewife at one level and at another it's she who wears pants in the family. She is the one who pushes her daughter to be out there in the world and fights for her to be treated as normal. *Amu* explored adoption and the complexities that arise between mother and child over that.

In *Margarita, With a Straw*, there is also a flip in the relationship of the carer and the cared. Both deal with the pain of loss of the mother.

Preeti: *Is the treatment of the protagonist from a sympathetic point of view of one of empowerment?*

Shonali: You never sympathize with the protagonist; you empathize with her. Even though she is disabled, she is created as a nuanced character with her own shades of grey. So it's impossible to pity her. Her journey is indeed empowering and leads her to a place of self love.

Preeti: *What was the most challenging aspect in depicting the protagonist's sexuality in the movie?*

Shonali: Shooting these scenes.

Preeti: *Because of your background and your involvement in activism, as well as your being a student of history, will there ever be a possibility of you making a movie that is not overtly political?*

Shonali: I have this position that there is no film that is not political. For instance, if you take even something like

Dilwale Dulhaniya Le Jaayenge or similar films, they are hard-core political because as soon as you are representing society, it is political. For example, what kind of family relationships are you showing, how are you representing gender? Any Hindi film, take the most stupid film that somebody thinks is not political, is so political. You have to look at the representation of caste, class and gender. You are not quote, unquote political in the sense that you are doing state terrorism, but the fact is that any representation is political. That is what sociology is, that is what the study of how anything is. How you are portraying politicians, how we reached this stage, how you are trying to say people are poor because they are lazy — in small ways, every film is political, even if made by the most hard-core Bollywood person. So, *Amu* was about state terrorism, *Chittagong* is on the freedom movement and *Margarita, With a Straw* is not that political, it's a personal story of sexuality. Sexuality is a very political thing, but in this film not in that typical way. I could make something which could be completely entertaining, but I would still consider it political. Say like *Khosla Ka Ghosla*, I still say it is a very political film, but many other people may not say that.

Nirmal: Are you ok about making a complete song-and-dance film?

Shonali: Complete song and dance *ka matlab kya hai*? There would have to be something in it that should interest me. If you are trying to say that it is not overtly political then yes, because for me I find it fascinating how you can embed so many little inputs and socio-political messages, which people don't get. I will always make intelligent cinema, but I don't mind making a film which is not overtly political. If I can write a script that is just about relationships, like a family drama, it would still remain political for me. If you're asking whether I will always address head-on political issues then no. It's just that I write what appeals to me.

Now it is the first time I am being asked to make a film not written by me, if it works out with these people. Hollywood has bought the rights for this one. So the Chitra Bannerjee Divakurni film is not a political book, but there are many interesting things that I find political. How will I treat it versus say Karan or Mira would be different because we'd each bring our own sensibility to it. I would be interested in making a mainstream film; it's just that three of my previous films have fallen into the circuit of film festivals, where they have been successes and they have had or will have a limited release. These films are for the urban class. Now, I would like to reach the masses. Therefore, I will have to make an entertaining film. But if we look at Prakash Jha's films, which are mass films and they are hard-core political films, I think the Indian audience is interested in politics per se.

What you're trying to say actually is that will I make a film with stars because that's the only difference. It's not that those are not political, for example, a Prakash Jha film. Big films are out there for the masses that are dealing with politics. I'm very open to such films also. There are actors who are stars, like Aamir. It immediately opens up a film to a huge audience. So I would be interested in reaching that huge audience. For that, you have to have a star. That's the sad fact. Luckily, there are stars today who can act. They are excited by different directors. Even if you see something like *Chak De! India*—Shah Rukh was fantastic. That's the perfect example of a film I would love to make. But you cannot say it's not political.

Nirmal: *What about something like* Swades?

Shonali: No. It was too preachy and too on the nose. I did not like it. I felt that it needed severe editing and that it was not a good film. But I loved *Chak de! India*. It seems to be just an effervescent and entertaining film, but it's really political. Look how it's dealing with gender, how it's dealing with the issue of the hockey team versus the cricket team, how it's dealing with the Muslim post-partition... all these issues. So it's just wonderfully entertaining, but so very political.

Source: Authors.

Director and screenwriter Anusha Rizvi belongs to a family of scholars and literary stalwarts. While her grandfather was none other than the illustrious Urdu poet Ghulam Rabbani Taban who had been the General Secretary of the Progressive Writers' Group, her father Professor Mujeeb Rizvi founded the Hindi Department at Jamia Millia Islamia University and is regarded as a leading academician of medieval poetry. Rizvi studied at Sardar Patel Vidyalaya, Delhi, and then read History at St. Stephen's, Delhi University. She worked at NDTV (New Delhi Television Limited) as a journalist and an assistant producer before jumping headlong into filmmaking. Rizvi met her husband, Mahmood Farooqui, at NDTV and they got married in 2002. Having had enough of the news media, Anusha eventually quit her job (her husband had already left McKinsey and worked at NDTV for just about a year), and so the two began their adventure with films.

Anusha Rizvi calls herself an accidental filmmaker. It was not until the end of 2005 that Rizvi hit upon a fruitful idea that would ultimately lead to the making of her debut film, *Peepli Live*. A news article reporting farmers' suicides in Andhra Pradesh compelled her to start writing the script for a movie, and it took Rizvi almost a year to complete it. A chance meeting with Aamir Khan's hair stylist set the ball rolling, and before she knew it Rizvi had sent her idea (her unfinished script) to Khan who then wanted to read the whole script. Very soon, Aamir Khan was on board as the film's producer.

Set in the fictitious state of 'Mukhya Pradesh', *Peepli Live* tells the story of brothers, Natha and Budhia, two harassed farmers buried in debt, and on the verge of losing their land and house to the bank. Frantic, the duo decides that Natha would commit suicide and in accordance with the state's policy, the family would receive compensation for his death. Word gets out, and jousting news channels desperate to film the suicide throw the life of the villagers in complete disarray. Not far behind, the local political parties attempt cashing in on the anticipated death. They all swoop down like hawks, each demanding their pound of flesh. A biting satire, the film dissects the rural–urban divide in India and lays bare the deep apathy prevailing towards the rural sectors as a whole.

Though city-bred, Anusha traces her familial roots back to Qaimganj in Uttar Pradesh, to a rural past of *zamindar*s steeped in communism. Perhaps, that is one reason she is not disconnected from the realities of the 'India' outside the major cities. Rizvi insists that the film is not just a commentary on the condition of farmers, but on the larger politics of misgovernance by the state as well as the lack of culpability of the media armed with its urban 'lens'. The director wishes to highlight the fact that a dead farmer is of more consequence to the government than one who is alive.

As a matter of fact, Rizvi specifies that both she and her co-director, her husband Mahmood Farooqui, were extremely conscious of the filming process in the village because they did not want to disrupt normal existence and the livelihoods of the local villagers. The last thing they wanted was to transform into the kind of intrusive and obsessive news channel reporters that they had portrayed in their own film.

Peepli Live was meant for the masses, the non-multiplex audience in small-town India, but it also became the toast of international film festivals. It was awarded the Best First Feature Film at the 31st Durban International Film Festival. It bridges the gap between two different worlds, but Rizvi is suspicious of the 'new wave cinema' tag. According to her, there is no cohesive or informed movement that is underway, and most Bollywood films are made for the urban viewer's sensibilities.

Content as King—How Stories Create Filmmakers

Preeti: *How did the transition from journalism to filmmaking happen?*

Anusha: I was not a working journalist when I was writing the script. I quit, and so it was not a continuous process. It was not a specific decision. It just so happened; at that time I was 27. Also, a while ago, in 2004, I had quit my job and I wasn't doing anything. I was thinking about where I wanted to head, and that's when this idea came to me and I decided to explore it a little. That's how.

Preeti: *Tell us a bit about your background and early life, and what kind of an upbringing you had.*

Anusha: Normal, I suppose (laughs). My father is a professor of Hindi. He taught medieval poetry. He is retired now. My mother used to work with the Soviet Embassy, but after the disintegration of the Soviet Union she left. So there was a whole bunch of people who left the Soviet Embassy, and she was one of them. I have one elder sister.

It is not a typical family unit. I didn't know my father's parents because they passed away before my father got married. So it has been my mother's parents, my *nana* and *nani*. I grew up with a lot of kids. Though we lived in separate houses, there was just one wall in the middle separating them. All the males were together. This was in Jamia, Delhi. Three of my *mamu*'s daughters also came to stay with us because he's a politician and he had to stay in his constituency as there was no education system there. Two of my *khala*s (mother's sisters) also stay in Delhi—so do their children. We were a bunch of kids who grew up together, and we were very, very, very fortunate to have the grandparents that we had and for the fact that our grandparents had the kind of time to spend with us—with each one of us. Each one of us had a very separate interaction with them, and very separate stories or memories of them.

Also, the housing systems were defined in such a way that we lived very close to each other. We still live very close to each other, almost walking distance. My parents' house is one block down, my sister stays here, and my cousins… we all sort of stick together. So it was that kind of a childhood.

Nirmal: *In a city like Delhi where you have the nuclear family as the norm, was it a disconnect?*

Anusha: When we were living in it, one didn't have that question because it was a lot more fun to be surrounded by so many women. Basically, we've grown up as five women together. If you were to see a unit, it would be—my mother, my father and the five of us, and our dog Talli who passed away three years ago. So that was our set up. That is the unit you're looking at, but it was a bit of a weird unit as we know it.

Nirmal: *Since you come from a joint family, was it difficult for you to meet other people who were living in nuclear families?*

Anusha: No, no. Why?

Nirmal: *Well, I've been living in Delhi for 21 years, and I see the joint family set up either in this area or in the Civil Lines area. The rest of the people have a disconnect and don't even understand it; for example, in my class my students don't even understand the concept of a joint-family system.*

Anusha: That's because you see my family has not migrated to Delhi, as in, we are not new settlers. In my case, there are many people of the same family who live close by. They've been living there for years. It's not like there has been a migration or an uprooting, or even if there was an uprooting, it was many, many years ago.

Preeti: *What was the value system of your family?*

Anusha: I have to again say that my family is a bit of a mix. It is a hugely political family, and other than the Bhartiya Janata Party (BJP) the family is divided into all parties. From Samajwadi to CPI(M), Communist Party of India (CPI), Congress, we are in everything. Also, my grandfather was not a card-holding Communist, but he was a sympathizer as was my grandmother. My father is a Gandhian, but he's a sympathizer. My mother is a card-holding Communist and both my *khala*s are card-holding CPI members. My *mamu*s are CPI(M) members. If you can understand the dynamics from this, you'd realize it's a very volatile situation.

My grandfather was also CPI, and that's how they all started together. He was also the general secretary of the Progressive Writers' Movement for the longest time. The house was very political where lots of people came—lots of poets, lots of writers, from the *Majaz*(s) to the *Faiz*(s). I remember Fahmida Riaz *ji*, a famous poetess from Pakistan, was exiled and she came to Jamia as India gave her asylum. She came to our house and stayed for many years. One saw exiled, political prisoners; one knew Pakistan, poetry, the Progressive Writers' Movement.

Preeti: *From a woman's perspective how was it — were there feminists in your house or were they, despite their political inclinations, still conservative in terms of their attitudes towards women?*

Anusha: When we were kids, we were told that we needed to have a career, needed to be independent and all of that was drilled into us. Besides that, all our mothers were working. One had that economic independence as a woman. Plus my grandmother was an extremely strong character in a lot of ways. Basically a very soft-spoken and polite person, but she controlled the entire set. So I've known very strong women in my life. But in retrospect, now I feel that... this whole concept of neo-feminism, which is that women should be independent, etc., has ended up putting much more pressure. Now no longer are you just women, you have to be superwomen. You have to do everything. You have to have a career, a marriage, children, a decent house — all of that.

I don't know if in retrospect I'll call their (family's) attitude conservative. I think it's tricky. And times are different. We are living in a very different society.

Nirmal: *Were you attracted towards communism? As a student, did you participate or join the communist movement?*

Anusha: Oh yes, of course. I can very easily say that we grew up on *dharna*s of all kinds. You are born in it. You know, there are two kinds of communists: those who read into it and those who are born into it. I'm the one who is born into it — I have no choice. I mean I've never felt strongly enough to be an official member and I don't think I'll ever become one, especially now.

Nirmal: *Didn't they try to persuade you to join the movement?*

Anusha: No, no. My father is a sympathizer, but very firmly a Gandhian.

Nirmal: *There is a kind of fraternal closeness in ideological terms between families in communism, and the green movement and feminism. Are you part of that kind of a set up? I see a kind of hyphenation between these three causes. One can switch between these three. Do you think that this is happening with the modern liberal situation today that Left-of-Centre could be a feminist, given a chance, could be a green activist, and at the same time he/she could be a communist as well? I mean did you inherit all these three ideologies?*

Anusha: First of all, there is no Left-of-Centre remaining in this country. The Left-of-Centre is now the Centre because the Left has changed its position and the Centre has not. The organized Left is a complete failure in this country and I am no part of it. But when we say 'Left', I do not wish to reduce it only to party politics. So these labels of feminism or communism do not work in this country anymore. Let's just first start to redefine. Then we can start labelling ourselves. But first and foremost let's redefine.

A West Bengal or a CPI(M) or a CPI... what's going on? What are their takes on partition, two-nation theory, today what they are doing in Nandigram? — I'm through with the organized Left, really.

Nirmal: *The Left or the communist ideology has influenced your thinking and that is reflected in your filmmaking as well.*

Anusha: Possibly, because all of that has formed me in every way. Even when I was two years old and didn't know anything, was taken to a *dharna*. I didn't know what it was, but I knew that there were those hundreds and thousands of people who were standing in the heat and asking for something desperately. You don't need to know what it is… it is something that forms you. I will not say that it was formed only by communist ideas because I have had a great influence of Gandhian ideas, more so now than in the past.

Preeti: *What has been the influence of Gandhian ideas on your life? Give us a few examples. Where do you see this influence, and how do you think this comes through?*

Anusha: You're asking me a very specific question. To me, social realities are understood very much by Gandhi. For instance, when we are looking at systems that do not recognize caste — we have to understand these things. When you're dealing with a country like ours, these are not quick solutions that we are looking for. We need to have a deeper thought about this country, these people.

Preeti: *Why did you choose to study History at St. Stephens?*

Anusha: Stephens was not my only choice. I applied only for History everywhere, and applied to five colleges. History because I like history, I've always liked history; it was assumed that I will study history because my *mamu* is a very well-known Historian and my *khalu* is another very well-known Historian.

Preeti: *When did you join college?*

Anusha: I joined college in 1994, and MBA was the big thing and economics.

Preeti: *Did you have any clarity about what you wanted to do after a degree in history?*

Anusha: I was very clear from the 10th standard. I had chosen the humanities because I liked the subjects. So I knew that whatever I would be doing would be within the set up of the liberal arts. And History is something I was strong at and liked, so it just made absolute sense. Political science and Sociology were not my things. In St. Stephens, I had only applied for History and not for Philosophy or English. It just so happened that year for some strange reason, 10 people were picked up from the same class in our school, Sardar Patel. Out of 40, 10 of us were in Stephen's.

Preeti: *So what sort of an experience was college? Who were the people who influenced your thinking the most, what was your friends circle like, and how active were you in college societies?*

Anusha: When you go to the college from a school like we were in, you are already a political, opinionated person. My school at that time, and I mean this as a compliment, had a reverse snobbery about things. We were the kids who didn't have a rock band, and we were the kids who would listen to Pandit Ravishankar in our holidays. We would be the kids who would read all the fancy books, and we would be the kids who would go and demonstrate when Babri Masjid.... Do you remember that exhibition where the Ram–Sita posters came out in Ayodhaya and there was all that beating up? We were the kids who got into trains and just rushed to Ayodhaya.

Coming from that kind of a school to St. Stephens ... you know. We didn't mind it so much because we were a bunch of women, and so it gives you a certain sense of confidence to know that all my friends, the entire group, we were all just picked up and put there. It also gives you a confidence that it's fine and we are acceptable. But the rest of the college didn't do anything. Basically, what they did was that en bloc they just blocked us, as in they never ragged us. We were just left alone as the women who were weird.

Preeti: *Especially in Delhi University, what I've seen is that wherever you do your Bachelor's from is basically your alma mater. Did you think that this was a disadvantage that all 10 of you came together, and so you remained in a ghetto?*

Anusha: No, no, I don't think it was a disadvantage at all. I am very grateful that something like that happened because frankly I didn't mind knowing those same women, and even today would still like to know them. They have turned out very well. We continued to have a relationship. For instance, I met Aditi and Ishita, two of my closest friends, in class 1. Then we thought we would be separated in college, but we weren't. So it's been a long journey as friends.

Preeti: *What about exposure? Were you able to branch out of that group and reach out to other people?*

Anusha: Well, yes. There are other people you start joining in. The first few weeks get over and you go for trips, you have assignments, you work with teachers, you're sitting in the café. Besides that we fought an election, so we had to get more people.

Preeti: *How active were you outside the History department and outside academics?*

Anusha: I was the cultural secretary for one year. I was also part of the History Society — we used to do tours and lectures.

Nirmal: *Was Stephen's — the Stephen's? At 64 you would still want to be called a Stephenian.*

Anusha: (Pauses) Yes. It was.

Nirmal: *So did Stephen's make a difference to your whole persona and growth? If yes, in what manner?*

Anusha: Though I'm not smitten by the brand, but yes, Stephen's does give you a sense of belonging. For example, let me show you something—this card, one of my teachers, Dr David Baker, sent to me a week ago. You can read it. He's just describing his research. This is what Stephen's does.

Preeti: Are you someone who has stayed in touch with your professors throughout?

Anusha: Some of them, but some have kept in touch with me, like Dr Baker.

Preeti: What did you do after your graduation?

Anusha: The option was Master's. I wanted to do a quick something during the summer, and my cousin Yasmin Menon who used to work with NDTV called me and said that there was an internship. I went there and I got the job. That's how I joined NDTV. I left them for a bit to do a course in human rights, it's implications, etc. After that again I applied to NDTV, got the job and joined back. I worked with NDTV for five years.

Nirmal: During that period you never thought of filmmaking.

Anusha: Not really. Not really, as me making a movie—no.

Nirmal: But you were not unaware of the technique. You were aware of the camera, the sound, recording and editing.

Anusha: For film, no. The cameras are very different for filmmaking, and the source material that you're working with, like whether it's digital video or film, they are different; like lighting is completely different. The one skill that I really picked up at NDTV and which has stood me in good stead so far is my editing skill. I am good at edits.

Courtesy: Kiran Rao.

That's a big advantage because when I am on the sets, I am able to think through the cut. Thankfully and because of which I feel, but maybe I am speaking too soon, we never had a reshoot in *Peepli Live*. We never ran short of footage, *ya beech mein kya lagega, aise kabhi nahin hua*. You know, we didn't have a patch. We had so much footage that we could do a five-hour movie.

Nirmal: *You come from a very established family, schooling, college and then a good job, and you suddenly decided to make a movie – or was it in the pipeline?*

Anusha: No, it was not in the pipeline at all. I met Mahmood at NDTV; at that time he wanted to make a movie. It wasn't very clear in my mind whether he wanted to make movies or he wanted to act in them. He was in NDTV for less than a year and then left to struggle it out in Mumbai. So I stayed on in Delhi and continued with my job. At that time, financially, it was difficult for both of us to quit at the same time.

Nirmal: *When did you get married?*

Anusha: 2002.

Nirmal: *What about the decision to pursue filmmaking? Wasn't it very sudden? It was a major decision to be making a big movie with a big production house and a film which was going to be a landmark film. So how did the idea come?*

Anusha: Yes, it was a sudden decision. Mahmood and I were hanging loose. I don't know how to make you understand this, as neither of us knew what we wanted to do. He had come back as a Rhodes Scholar from Cambridge. He had these ideas about wanting to start theatre in India and only work in India, having given up this fancy McKinsey job. We were like *India mein karna hai, kya karna hai, kaise karna hai. Karna hi kya hai yehi nahin pata tha.* I was not really clear... which is why I keep saying that I am very accidental as a filmmaker. I have no skill, no training, and I do not have a style because I am such an accidental, random entrant into filmmaking.

Preeti: *So a person who has no idea of filmmaking, no idea of technique, no published work, no documentary filmmaker suddenly graduates into filmmaking. How were you accepted into the film fraternity? Was it not daunting for you? Did it not scare you in the beginning?*

Anusha: I am telling you how it happened, so you figure it out. There was a friend of ours, who had started seeing this girl in Mumbai. So he brought her to Delhi for us to meet. She happened to be Aamir Khan's hair stylist, Avan Contractor. So we got talking over dinner, and this is just a random meeting of friends to introduce a girlfriend and she said, 'You have a great idea, and why don't you write to Aamir?'

Preeti: *So by that time had you already written the script that was called* The Falling?

Anusha: No, I had the idea and I was just beginning to put it down on paper, and that too on a register, handwritten.

Preeti: *And this was when you had quit your job and your husband was struggling in Bombay.*

Anusha: No. By then, we had both returned to Delhi. In 1999, he went to Bombay and by 2002 we got married and came back to Delhi. We both didn't like Bombay at all and decided to come back to Delhi. We were in Bombay for just six months.

Nirmal: *So someone made a suggestion to you that you should meet Aamir Khan. Didn't you think that it was improbable. I mean why would he talk to you because there are so many people who have great ideas and they want to make a film with Aamir Khan or Yash Chopra as a producer.*

Anusha: Yes, exactly, which is why I did not run to Bombay to meet him. I just sent him an email. I did not have Aamir's email, and so she gave me his email address. *Phir wo baat khatam ho gayi.* Then a day or two later, we thought why not give it a try... you never know. So randomly, I wrote him a mail saying that this is what I have studied, this is where I have worked and I have an idea. And I asked him whether he wants to see it. So we just left it at that. Then I realized the next morning that he had replied. Basically, he wrote back saying that we should send him the full script and he would look at it. But we didn't have the full script. So because he had asked for it, I had to finish the script. I finished it. It took me three months to write it.

Preeti: *So you finished the script in three months or was this the screenplay?*

Anusha: I didn't know any difference between a screenplay and script. I knew only the story and how it is to be seen. I knew *ki yeh itna dikhana chahiye iss time pe, aur saath mein koyi yeh bolna chahiye, aur iss aadmi ko side-face se yeh bolna chahiye.* I didn't know how to write it down. So all these fancy final drafts I didn't have. I just had a word processor. *Toh jaise bhi us mein likha gaya,* I wrote it. I still write like that.

Anyhow, I sent him the script. I think he was shooting at that time and he didn't reply for a few months. After that, he asked for it again and I sent it to him. I was working at that time with a company called Mediatech to do a documentary on the hijacking of IC-184. I was shooting for that at Mr Dobal's house at Noida, and my light guys wanted a day off the next day because Aamir Khan's shooting was to take place in Delhi.

What I found out later was that at that time, he had come to do the publicity for *Mangal Pandey: The Rising.* So when he got my mail which was titled *The Falling*, he assumed that I was pulling his leg about his movie, which was why he read my mail in the first place. So I wrote him a mail that evening saying that I knew he would be in Delhi, as my light boys had told me, and that if he wanted me to give them off he should meet me for that period. He didn't reply. The next morning, at six, he called to say that he could give me an hour and a half or so. I think even then he was thinking it was just a grand joke or something. Anyhow, I was shooting, but I reached, and so I was a little late as I had got stuck. I just had pointers with me, so I read those out, what the story would be without dialogues. He was quiet and didn't react at all. So I asked him what he thought and he said that he would get back to me. This was 2005. Then there were these series of meetings over the whole year, which is when I was called to Bombay and asked to narrate the script to various people—to his manager, to Kiran, to Prasoon Joshi and others.

Preeti: *Were you given any amount for the shots that had to be set up for the test?*

Anusha: They provided us with ₹2 lakhs for everything, but that's a very small amount of money when it comes to shooting. You have to hire talent and location. Even if you're shooting for two days, you have to provide food: three meals a day for all the 100 people who are there. So it was a very tight budget; anyhow we managed to shoot it. And Akshat and Jim were supposed to shoot their test for *Taare Zameen Par*, although the decision had already happened because Aamir had taken over. Abbas was badly caught because his pre-production was already done and his movie was once stopped with Vashu Bhagnani. So for two times, he had spent a year each doing pre-production for different production houses. Now at this stage, he was being told that he had to test! He also tested, but he only tested on film, as in he shot through the film camera. We both did it as a video thing in which *Peepli Live* got approved and *Delhi Belly* was rejected. All this happened in November 2006. *2007 humne* Taare Zameen Par *ka wait karne mein lagaya aur 2008 ke end tak humne wait kiya.*

Preeti: *What were you doing in this period?*

Anusha: We were doing *Dastangoi* and other things—you do whatever comes your way.

Preeti: *You had not lost hope with this film. What was the gut feeling that told you that you would do this film?*

Anusha: No, I hadn't surprisingly.
I don't know, but I had a feeling.

Nirmal: *Since there was no assurance, did you ever go to other production houses?*

Anusha: I did try... at one point, only once in 2007, when we were continuously waiting and there was no definitive answer coming from anywhere. We tried to approach Prakash Jha — once — during this whole process.

Nirmal: *Considering that your script was a script bordering on being an art film script (without chart-popping songs or major actors) completely different from the other three films Aamir Khan was producing, or for that matter any big producer was producing, how did you feel that he would accept such a film? Do you think that on your part also it was a somewhat crazy idea to have thought of such a script? — I mean you didn't think of doing a candyfloss romance.*

Anusha: No, but that was the idea that I had sent to Aamir in the first place. It wasn't as if I wanted to make movies generically. I had an idea and it was that idea I wanted to turn into a movie. I didn't want love stories or anything else. That's it. I wasn't interested in any other story except for this one.

Nirmal: *I was talking to one director who said that he always had two or three scripts ready, and if the producer didn't like one he would fish out another.*

Anusha: I know, I know. A lot of people work like that. It's not a question of right or wrong. It's just a question of speed. Perhaps, I'm just slow at telling a story. But I don't have scripts ready beforehand.

Preeti: *So which year did you start shooting your film, finally?*

Anusha: In 2009.

Nirmal: *So you got a final yes then. Did he talk to you again?*

Anusha: See, we got a 'yes' in 2005. Every two months it was a final yes. There was never a 'no' from Aamir from day one. I always felt that the film would be made, call it whatever you want. It just was a matter of clicking and he found the film really, really funny. He really liked it. There was no reason for me to feel that I shouldn't make it because I had a producer and I had a script. Why shouldn't I have made it?

Nirmal: *I am intrigued. Did it never cross your mind that you were a journalist with no idea of filmmaking and why would any production house make films with you? Yours was not a commercial script and to go ahead with such a decision would require guts.*

Anusha: I had a producer. Why would I think about this when I already have one? Whatever Aamir's thought process was, I cannot answer that—I don't know. Why he decided to do this and what would have worked for him—I don't know. For me what worked was that he came across as a very, very nice guy, he was very polite, he gave you respect, he heard you out and he had no problems with the script. It was fantastic, in the sense that he never asked me to make changes or hold back.

You know all filmmakers will tell you that no matter who you are, if you have an opportunity to make a film, you should make it. I had that opportunity.

Nirmal: *Were you not tempted to take stars because none of your characters, except one or two, are cinematically known to us?*

Anusha: But that's the whole idea. Why would I.... I don't like stars. Who would have played Natha? I cannot imagine anyone within the current star list. Besides, it's not a very democratic industry. It's not like Hollywood where you have a number of A-listers where you can pick from. We have three A-listers, and so it is more of a monopoly. What are we talking about? There are hardly any male stars! And what will you do with the female stars?

Nirmal: *Did you ever imagine that it would be such a huge success even commercially?*

Anusha: For me the more important thing was that I was getting to tell this story—this very story that I wanted to tell and the manner in which I wanted to tell it, with absolutely no compromise on my politics and what I wanted to say in it. The rest can only be decided because filmmaking is not a small process; it is a process that is so long drawn out that if you start thinking at the idea stage that this will be a great movie... I don't know. I don't care, frankly. At the idea stage, it should appeal to me. I don't care about the rest of the world.

Nirmal: *Your movie's commercial reception was superb. Generally, such a movie doesn't get such a release, you know, the 'film festival' kind of films.*

Anusha: You say that, but what do you mean? How many screens was it released in? It doesn't work like that. You have a similar release pattern for almost all films. Initially, you release 150 prints. That's when the first-day release happens in major cities. Then you start getting distribution demands. Once the distributor has seen the film and has seen the first reaction of the first day that's when other distributors who have not bought your film start to call you for it. That's when you're prepared. Instead of 150 prints, you give 200 prints and more *agar aur demand aati hai. Aur phir chhotte centres mein demand aane lagti hai, aapka Benaras hai, Bhopal hai, yahaan, wahaan, to phir aap aur badhate ho.* It is not as if you begin by saying that *ki main film 700 prints mein release karoonga.* The film was released in 150 prints like most other films, that is, small movies. *Uss mein distributor ki demand aayi tab aapne print badhaya na.* Delhi Belly ko zyada bada release kiya tha, main maanti hoon. Dhobi Ghat ko 600 prints mein release kiya tha. Mera 150 prints release kiya tha – sabka aisa hota hai. I think Tere Bin Laden ka 150 hua tha. All these small films have 150 prints – regular.

Preeti: *So how long did it take for you to shoot the whole film and finish the post-production work? What were the challenges?*

Anusha: In actuality, I can't really define the time period because the time was very, very flexible according to how and when Aamir was available. *Film shoot karne mein humko 64 days lage. Phir hum March ke end tak shoot karke, 25th March ko waapis aa gaye. 10th April ko humne edit shuru kiya. 10th April se 29th May ko, 2009 mein, first edit complete ho gaya.* I have all these diary listings. *29th May ko woh Aamir ne pehli baar dekha.* He said that 80% was done and that he loved it.

Uske baad May se le kar September tak there was no work on the scene. *Uske alag, alag, reasons the. Uss mein,* very unfortunately, Kiran had a miscarriage, and so it took them a while to get over that. They had to go away. Then when he came back, he had other commitments and plus in that year he was shooting *Three Idiots. Toh uska shoot chal raha tha. Uss dauraan, August–September mein kuch nahi hua, hum baithe rahe. Kuch ho nahin sakta jab tak edit lock nahi hai – sound nahin ho sakta, colour correction nahin, kuch nahin ho sakta.* Then Aamir decided that instead of sitting on *Peepli Live*'s edit, he wanted to sit on *Delhi Belly's* edit because that was shot first. But *Delhi Belly ke edit mein bahut time lagne wala tha,* so I begged him to see *Peepli Live* and he agreed. Then he sat on the edit for 10 days, during which we fought and fought like cats and dogs.

But the problem was that in the meantime, the production house missed the deadlines for the film to be entered into festivals. So we passed all the deadlines. The Berlin Committee had come to watch the film and they really liked it. The Sundance we missed completely. Then, somehow, Aamir managed to send a DVD through a guy in the US to John. He saw the film and he decided to stop the Sundance committee. He called and he said that we were in. That's how we got to Sundance. But Sundance begins by the 9th of January, and until the first week of December no work had been done on the film. No sound, no music, nothing. But we were in a competition. We were not some random film, but were competing with 13 other films within the world. And we had done nothing, no technical work.

Ek mahine mein hua woh sab. It was a fairly shoddy job, and it just hugely took down the film technically. We didn't have time to change the print because in February the Berlin Film Festival begins, so the same print went there as well. There were glaring mistakes in the print, like spelling mistakes in the subtitles. Sound was bad, in some portions the video was dark—*chehra nahi dikhayi deh raha tha character ka.* It was unbelievably bad stuff that went out to those festivals. Nobody had time in the production house to think that this was an important film or that one will be able to gain something out of it. So, in a way, we missed out on two major film festivals.

Aamir was in hiding for 15 days for the promotion of *Three Idiots.* He hid till the 25th of December. And it is he who has to take calls on things like final designs for posters; he has to sign cheques for the money. He was the producer of the film. He was the owner. And he was not there. He was in hiding, and I couldn't get in touch with him.

Maybe for other directors the timing was fine, but for me the timing was really bad. In a week's time, we had to leave for Sundance. This hiding was supposed to be some very secret affair, and the whole nation was looking for him. The media had started following him. For instance, his bodyguards were not allowed to reveal to their families where they were. *Woh kitna successful hua ya nahi hua* I don't know because I was fully involved with the movie. *Producer nahi hai ek hafta pehle available, toh nahi hai.*

Nirmal: *You took all the cameras, lights, cables to the village. For you, these technicalities must have been difficult – the whole filmmaking process.*

Anusha: In the process in which we were trying to help the villagers into gradually accepting all that, which being in a film entails, like *unki poori livelihood hi khatam ho jaati hai*, we had to be careful in gradually allowing this stuff—so non-organic—machines, and all of that; as we were doing that, we too were slowly getting used to the idea of these machines, the lights, etc. Of course, if you've dealt with media you know lights and camera. The difficult part is that when you go onto the set for the first time and you look around and there are, in our case 500 people, the whole of the village is there, and they're just all looking for you to take your first command. That takes a while—to grow in confidence with your commands, even when you know what you want, but having to voice it in front of all these people who are standing and watching you. It takes a while, may be two or three days, and then the film takes over, characters take over, the work takes over. You have no time. You are exhausted.

Courtesy: Onir.

Born to a Bengali couple, Aparesh and Manjushree Dhar, and named Anirban, filmmaker Onir spent his early childhood years in Bhutan. Introduced to a range of Indian cinema at a tender age, he soon cultivated a deep love for films that eventually paved the way for a distinctive brand of filmmaking. It was Shyam Benegal's *Junoon* that left an indelible mark on the young boy's mind and crystallized the dream of working with cinema. Ethnic conflict in Bhutan forced the Dhar family to migrate to India, and Onir left his first home never to return. This sense of exile would come to haunt his films and the subjects he would choose to portray.

An autonomous spirit from the very start, Onir chose West Bengal's Jadavpur University over the science college his parents were keen on. Here, Onir pursued a course in comparative literature and simultaneously completed a course in filmmaking from Chitrabani. After the academic stint at Calcutta, he gained a scholarship in 1994 to study advanced film editing at the Television Training Centre of Sender Freies in Berlin.

Onir's filmic influences covered both world cinema, from Godard to Tarkovsky, as well as Indian cinema, represented by artists such as Satyajit Ray and Ritik Ghatak. Inspired by a certain form of cinema and fuelled by radical ideologies, albeit within the confines of Bollywood, the soon-to-be director was already up against a wall with his very first film. The journey he set out on has proven to be an arduous but rewarding one.

Between 1999 and 2004, Onir did all the customary rounds, determined to finance his first script (*My Brother Nikhil*) without having to compromise either on the story or his treatment of it. After failed attempts to secure a like-minded producer, friend and actor Sanjay Suri suggested that Onir produce the film himself.

Backed by Suri, family and well-wishers, the filmmaker made his debut feature, *My Brother Nikhil* (2005). It is based on the real-life experience of homosexual AIDS patients in the eighties who are shunned by the government, their loved ones and the society in general. Without sensationalizing, the director tells a fictional story of a swimming champion, Nikhil (Sanjay Suri), struggling with AIDS, of his fiercely supportive sister Anu (Juhi Chawla), his loving boyfriend Nigel and the disintegrating familial and social relations that surround them.

Onir travelled with *My Brother Nikhil* to many international queer film festivals, where it received accolades and a wider audience than it did in India. Back home, while critics praised the film for its integrity, it remained confined to a small viewership.

Though candid about his own sexual orientation, Onir dismisses labels that render him a gay director. He has maintained that his cinema highlights repressed stories, homosexuality being one such critical reality, though not the only one.

Next, in 2006, Onir released *Bas Ek Pal*, a film dealing with the emotional embroilment of five troubled characters whose entwined stories begin to unravel dangerously. Boasting a cast that included seasoned actors like Juhi Chawla and Urmila Matondkar, Onir's second venture received a lukewarm response, as did his third film, the romance, *Sorry Bhai* (2008).

It was a collation of four individual stories that became *I Am* (2011), Onir's crowd-funded fourth endeavour. Opening up issues (artificial insemination, bigotry, child abuse) that are usually silenced in India, this quartet is a tribute to human dignity and selfhood.

The irony is that though *I Am* received two National Film Awards and Onir was forced to cut out certain scenes, the film is still unavailable to the vast majority because it cannot be telecasted on Doordarshan. Despite the odds, the tenacious filmmaker continues to remain true to his art.

The Politics at the Margins—Being an Alternative Filmmaker in Bollywood

Preeti: *What was it like growing up in Bhutan? How did you get into movie making?*

Onir: I was born and brought up in Bhutan. My parents were teachers. My father was a principal and my mother was a teacher. I have a younger brother and an elder sister.

Bhutan is an extremely small country. At that time, the population was about 25,000 in the capital city where I used to live. Once a week we used to go for movies. That was our only entertainment. My mother, being a major film buff, used to drag us and while we would pretend that we didn't want to go. My father was not so inclined towards movies.

Apart from that, we spent a great deal of time doing a lot of outdoor activities, like gardening, fishing and hiking. We grew up reading a lot of books too, not watching TV; I never saw TV till I was in class 10 when I came to India for winter vacations. That's when I saw TV for the first time. So it was a childhood minus TV, and I'm very, very happy that it was that way.

We also grew up in a family... which I feel extremely fortunate, where all of us in were treated the same, in the sense that my father would make breakfast and one of us would help; my mother would make lunch and the other one would help. All of us grew up learning to cook, do our own stuff, and it was normal for us to watch both my parents cook and do the household work. So for me, it was a cultural shock when I first came to Calcutta for higher studies, and went to Jadavpur University to do my comparative literature. I suddenly realized that I was not even aware of what eve-teasing was, for example, in Bhutan. But when we came to Calcutta, I suddenly noticed how my elder sister would be harassed everywhere because she was wearing a pair of jeans. And I realized that though we grew up in a very small town, we were much more liberal in the way we thought and in the gender equations, specially, which were so warped in Calcutta. That was my first experience in India, and then I realized that like in most places in India, it was not balanced at all.

When I was in school, at that point, we used to watch all kinds of movies. My mother took us to watch *Deewar* or *Sholay*; at the same time we watched *Akrosh, Mandi, Bhumika* and *Junoon*. And I'm glad… because my father was the Principal and though we were children, the gatekeeper would never stop us because literally everyone was a student. I don't think it affected any of us negatively because my parents always spoke and explained things to us. When I was in class 8, I saw Shyam Benegal's *Junoon*, and I didn't understand the film. But the visual impression, which that film made (or a film like *Aakrosh*) made at that age, made me want to be a part of cinema. As young as that, I knew that I wanted to be a part of films.

Preeti: *Before you decided to pursue literature at Jadavpur, what sort of expectations did your parents have in terms of your career choices?*

Onir: Well, my parents initially wanted me to be a doctor. I had this dream that, initially, before this filmmaking, was subconsciously there... first I thought that I wanted to be a pilot, anything to do with travelling, then a sailor; I had all these romantic ideas about flying. But by the time I was in class 12, I knew it was not my cup of tea.

In school, I used to barely pass... the pass mark was 36; I remember it was maths, I would answer till 40 and leave the hall because it didn't matter, it didn't interest me at all. Physics was the only thing that kind of interested me. My mother was very keen that I became a doctor. So from Bhutan, they admitted me into a science college and they left, and I applied to Jadavpur for comparative literature. I shifted without telling them when I got in. After my name was struck out of the other college, that's when I told them that was in Jadavpur.

Jadavpur was one of the best things that could happen to me because not only was I doing something, I mean I love literature, I also knew it would take me closer to what I wanted to do. Parallely, I started doing film studies at Chitrabani. Jadavpur had an extremely active film society. Comparative literature was more like comparative arts. One was talking about films, poetry, painting and different forms of art. Suddenly, I just felt engulfed in this atmosphere where everyone was interested in cinema and literature. I was a part of the film society; so we would just go up to the archive constantly, get the films one wanted to see and organize festivals. At that time, unlike now, the International Film Festival of India used to be a travelling festival. So when they used to come to Calcutta we would queue up from the night before so that we would get tickets.

There was this excitement in Calcutta. Parallely, I started learning Russian, German because... just to see more films. I was involved in a whole lot of activities, but at the same time knowing that ultimately I want to make films. Because at that point, you needed to be a graduate before you could apply to FTII for formal training. So not only was Jadavpur giving so much of exposure, as a place also it was much more open. I remember the college I was admitted to first was a Calcutta University college, and the first day when I went there the SFI Union caught hold of me and said, 'Why are you wearing torn jeans? Are you a drug addict?' Then next thing my professor tells me, 'Oh! You're wearing a pink t-shirt. Your parents have not taught you anything.' Then I realized that the girls were sent back if they wore *salwar kameez*. You could only wear *sarees*. It was that regressive a college. I was there for a month before I shifted to Jadavpur University. So for me, coming to Jadavpur University was elating. Nobody cared, and people were much more open-minded and much more progressive. It was a nice atmosphere.

That's when my sister finished her graduation and went off to FTII to study as an editor. As I finished my graduation, I applied to FTII. I didn't get through FTII, but a week later I got a scholarship to go and study film editing in Berlin. So I went to Berlin to train in editing. I was glad that it was editing because I knew that I didn't really want to work as an assistant, but wanted to be the head of a department. As a person, I'm pretty independent, it wouldn't have been easy for me to make my films. So it was good if I learned some craft and start using that to slowly get into the industry. So I went to Berlin to learn filmmaking.

Nirmal: *From Jadavpur to Berlin. Why Jadavpur? You came from Bhutan. Was it only because it was in Bengal? You didn't choose any other place.*

Onir: No, initially at one point I wanted to go to Darjeeling. My sister was studying at Lady Brabourne, Calcutta, and I'm very, very close to her. I was very sure that if she was in Calcutta then I would come to Calcutta. So it was more to do with the fact of being with my sister that I came to

Calcutta. But I wanted to do literature, and particularly comparative literature.

Preeti: *In fact, I think there are very few places in India where comparative literature is offered.*

Onir: At that point, it was only Jadavpur. JNU or Hyderabad University didn't have it.

Preeti: *What was the duration of the programme in Berlin?*

Onir: First, it was like a three-month advanced course and then it spread over one-and-a-half years where I was working with different directors, doing workshops with them outside in other places.

Preeti: *So when you came back to India, was there a lot of struggle involved in getting into the industry?*

Onir: I came back in 1992 and, first, I wanted to continue working in Calcutta. I was very attached to the city. I had saved money from my scholarship, and I made my first documentary in Calcutta on a painter called Bijon Chaudry, who had passed away. The documentary was called *Fallen Heroes*. It was about a series of his paintings. So like all Bengalis, it was a lot of painting and poetry. At that point the only outlet, I suppose even now, for documentary was Doordarshan. But you couldn't get anything shown there without bribing and that was not my cup of tea. So I never got shown anywhere except for a few film festivals.

I was trying to work in Calcutta, but it was extremely difficult because I was very young and everyone had this *dada* attitude. Also I was trained abroad, people were somewhat hostile. By then my sister had passed out of FTII and had shifted to Bombay. So she said, 'Why don't you come over?' I got a job as an editor and I shifted to Bombay in 1994.

Nirmal: *How much of an impact did Jadavpur or your Berlin experience have on your early filmmaking?*

Onir: I feel that there are three different parts to me as a filmmaker. One is the place where you are born, which makes you the person you are in terms of your basic values. College, Jadavpur, basically enabled me to evaluate things beyond the surface.... It just opened up the window to the world. Being able to question things came with Jadavpur.

In Berlin, what I learned was not only the craft, but also 'discipline'. You stick to time, you plan—so much more of the practical side of it. That really helped me as an independent filmmaker because I was shooting with low budgets, time constraints. I've always finished films within budget, within schedule because there's a lot of pre-planning, and I'm very particular about time.

Nirmal: *But does Bombay work like that?*

Onir: Bombay, not the old school mainstream cinema. But increasingly, the younger filmmakers—if you're not working within the 'star' system, are getting much more organized. People are valuing time, money and effort, much more.

Nirmal: *The initial days you were talking about films like* Junoon *and* Aakrosh, *but you didn't see much of world cinema at that time.*

Onir: Not in Bhutan, but the minute I came to Calcutta, I stopped watching Hindi films. Hindi films disappeared from my life when I came to Calcutta, and all I used to watch was world cinema. Not even Hollywood. I stopped watching Hollywood also. It was just mostly European cinema. I became a huge fan of new wave European cinema. I started watching a lot of Bengali films. I identify with European cinema more.

Nirmal: *What is European for you? You're talking of Italian films.?*

Onir: No, I'm talking of the entire new wave European cinema. If you look at French cinema—Godard, Renoir, Alain Resnais—I used to love watching those films.

Nirmal: *Have they impacted your filmmaking?*

Onir: I don't know if directly, but a lot of people say it's quieter and closer to that in terms of that everything is not loudly pronounced. So I think, yes, in a certain way. At the same time, it is also influenced by Bengali filmmakers like Satyajit Ray, Ritik Ghatak, who are amazing… they are in the same space as world cinema. I watched Iranian, Russian films. I love Tarkovsky. I saw a lot of films. Bergman. You name it. We just saw films, films and films. I don't know how many films at times one watched in a day, at that time.

Nirmal: *Your films, compared to European cinema, if we look at them from the lighting point of view, have well-lit frames, what I call 'happy' frames. That is a very conscious effort on your part to keep all the frames well lit. They are very different from what you're calling European new wave cinema. You don't make dark films.*

Onir: You have not seen my films carefully. They are not well lit. If you have seen then you wouldn't say that. There are huge sequences in *My Brother Nikhil* where you don't even see the characters. They are shot in the night, by the sea, where all you see is almost like shadows. And that's what people in Europe loved, while in India a lot of people found it dark. You can't see faces. Even in *I Am,* it is not well lit. There's a lot of darkness. They are not like Hindi films where there's flat bright lighting, not at all. Some of the critics have talked about the beauty of the sea sequences in the night when you just didn't see the characters. It was like shadows.

Sorry Bhai, because the film was a romantic, bright film, is totally different. The lighting of the film is dependent not just on what I would like, but also on what the content demands.

Nirmal: *I was talking about this film yesterday to Dibakar and we agreed that somebody had copied your film, frame-by-frame, and made big bucks. How do you feel when somebody doesn't give you credit and makes a film?*

Preeti: *How is copyright implemented in the industry? What's the new scenario?*

Onir: For one, our legal system is so screwed up. It depends on who can hire the more expensive and influential lawyer. It's such a long, expensive procedure that as an independent filmmaker, like for me, either you make a film or spend time in the court. They have their representatives, while I would have to sit there myself. It just does not work for me.

And also, in India, if you change five lines... that is enough.

Nirmal: *Imitation is the best form of flattery. If only you had included big stars and a lot of songs.*

Let's come back to the first film that you made, My Brother Nikhil. *When you approached the producer for this film, didn't you find it difficult, with such a subject, a new director and new stars except Juhi Chawla? What problems did you face?*

Onir: The reason that we produced it ourselves is because no one else would produce it. Initially, we went to many producers and it was very simple that either you make Nikhil's character heterosexual or get Bipasha Basu to give Nikhil AIDS or change Juhi Chawla to Yana Gupta. All these kinds of suggestions and for me becoming a director were not so important to make the film that I want; to make my film was much more important. So finally, we decided we'd do it ourselves. Friends, family, we all got together.

Nirmal: *Were you happy with the reaction that the film got?*

Onir: For me, it was very clear that I want to be a filmmaker. At the same time, I didn't know whether I was good or bad. But I thought that when I make my first film and when I watch it, if I respect what I do then I can continue; otherwise I'll quit and do something else. Box office is never something that motivates me or drives me. Of course, if it makes it, one feels good but it's never been the driving force about selecting what I want to do.

When *My Brother Nikhil* released, of course, it was critically acclaimed in India and travelled a lot abroad. I've travelled to so many countries with the film, and I still travel. It's been theses and papers for lots of students. I was at a conference in Shimla and there were two people who presented their theses on *My Brother Nikhil*. It was kind of odd because I was sitting in the conference and suddenly I hear them. They were also feeling awkward that they are dissecting the film.

I constantly take classes on Skype with universities and sometimes travel in the US for *My Brother Nikhil*. Though it didn't get recognition in the country, I have travelled the world with this film. It's a very special film for a lot of people... a lot of NGOs, a lot of people from the lesbian gay bisexual and transgender (LGBT) community. I get SMSes and emails even now about that film. It gave me my identity as a filmmaker. When I came here, people knew that this is Onir and he makes films with a certain sensibility.

Preeti: *I have watched* My Brother Nikhil, Sorry Bhai *and most recently* I Am, *and now I am talking to you and understanding*

Brave New Bollywood

Courtesy: Onir.

the sort of sensibility and cultural milieu that you come from. Help me understand why you chose a subject like Sorry Bhai? *Was it some sort of a yearning to get back to mainstream cinema and make romantic films?*

Onir: As a director, it is very important to do different forms of cinema. Otherwise you stop growing if you keep doing the same kind of film. As a filmmaker, I love watching romances. I would love to do a romance or an adventure film as long as the story is not regressive. So for me *Sorry Bhai* was an attempt where you do what is perceived as a usual commercial film, but at the same time there are a lot of things which are consciously done that are not regressive. For me, it's as commercial as it can get. But when the film released, I remember, there were comments like 'Oh! Onir is known for pushing the envelope but there's a limit'. or 'It's a sin to watch this movie'. It was again considered to be an offbeat film.

But people missed out small things. For me the girl, she was Aaliyah, a Muslim girl. It was very important for me that she was a Muslim girl without any codified identity and for whom religion never plays....

Nirmal: *Girls' parents' reluctance to come... that's the only give away.*

Onir: Even Shabana does not bring up religion as a problem because I don't want it. It's just normal.

Preeti: *In* Sorry Bhai, *which is otherwise a progressive film, there is this obsession with* maa kasam. *Why?*

Nirmal: *Even in* My Brother Nikhil, *there is a yearning for the parents and their approval.*

Onir: I think there are two things. Sometimes we don't treasure, actually, what is beautiful about being in a family. For me, it's extremely precious, just like friendship. Everything can only happen with a dialogue and the *maa kasam* thing with the brother, for me is fun because he's a scientist. It's like playing a game and when you grow up you don't believe it, but you feel that if something happens then what.

My own sister, an extremely progressive woman, swore upon her daughter that she would quit smoking. After that she's just not been able to because even though she doesn't believe that anything will happen to her daughter she won't be able to forgive herself if it does. So it is not superstition, but more to do with a kind of belief that you've grown up with, and you care for a person and you don't want anything to happen to them.

Secondly, I feel that it's very easy to be non-inclusive. The entire idea of the LGBT community... why is it fighting for acceptance? It's very easy for just everyone to go to the US. I would hate to show that. Like they do it in the serial *Maryada*... you go away to the US because you're not accepted in this country. The idea is to fight, make a change and be accepted. Today, *My Brother Nikhil* is very special for a lot of people because, unlike in the West, family is important and I think there's nothing wrong with it. I think it's lovely to be able to have a support system as long as you're able to have that dialogue. It's much better for children to be able to grow up with grandparents than being dumped in nurseries where you're brought up without any personal touch. You're brought up like 10 other kids. I feel fortunate that I've grown up with my grandfather's stories. At the same time I'm extremely independent. I have grown up with my family. At the same time I do what I want to do. And I feel that's because I have a dialogue with my family. So I feel that acceptance opens up and it's not just a question of family. In India, the family is such a strong fabric that once you are accepted by them, you can fight rest of the world. So for *My Brother Nikhil*, it is very important that once Nikhil is accepted, it sends out a much larger social message. Today, a lot of women, when they want to marry someone outside their community, would give a damn about society if they had their family's support. It is because of lack of support from the father, brother and the fear of loss of family because you've grown with these people whom you can't just reject because now there is someone else in your life. Very often one makes compromises, but these films are not about making compromises, but about bringing change in people.

Onir

Courtesy: Onir.

Preeti: *But don't you feel that this romanticization of the family then inhibits you as a director from looking at the politics of family itself as a social institution?*

Onir: The politics of the family played a huge part in *My Brother Nikhil*. Right from the brother-sister relationship, how the father treats the son and daughter in different ways and how the mother does not have a say, but at the end she puts her foot down. At the same time, the paternal hierarchy and the father constantly refusing to believe and the last thing is his moulding, him accepting. He does not even accept his son's sexuality till the son is dead.

Why does the sister refuse to go back to the house? That is her rebellion. She says that she will not go back to that house, and only goes back when the brother is nearly dying and at his last request. But till then she does not step into that house. There is constant defiance.

The father/husband says that everybody stop talking to him. Though he's holding on to his power, but his wife and daughter have stopped interacting with him and he has lost his son. There are doors being closed on him because people are not accepting the power structure. So it is questioning the entire politics of family.

You come to a film like *I Am*, where the entire family structure is broken up. So it depends again on the story and what is important. Nandita, at the end, breaks the so-called family idea. The character of Abhimanyu in the child-abuse piece questions the entire family idea. If you see the other two stories, the family ideal is questioned. Actually, in the last one, family does not exist at all.

Nirmal: *What kind of preparation do you make for your films? Are you a bound-script kind of person or do you improvize?*

Onir: I like to do a lot of preparation, but at the same time, when I go to the set I tell my actors that this is the space, I want you to walk from here to here, this is the dialogue, this is how I see my shot, but also ask the actor how they would like to do it. Suppose an actor wants to improvize and it's better for the film then I change my shot as necessary. If I'm not convinced then I convince him/her.

Preeti: *Can you give us a couple of instances where this has happened in some significant frames?*

Onir: I'll give you two examples from *Sorry Bhai* itself. There's a sequence where the character of Chitrangada is confiding in Shabana and they're in a tent in the night and they hug, and Chitrangada starts crying. So this was the first day of the shoot when both were working together, and Chitrangada was highly stressed. And when we started rehearsing for the shot, she told me that she just didn't feel like hugging Shabana. It wasn't coming to her naturally. So Shabana looked at me and said that even she didn't think it was necessary. Since both my actors felt so strongly about it, I agreed. So we started shooting and the scene did nothing to me. It didn't work for me, and I asked them to hug each other. They did the scene the way I wanted it and before I could say anything, Shabana looked at me and said, 'You were right.'

There was another scene with Boman and Sharman, and I was trying to figure out the shot, etc. Boman came to me and suggested that the entire scene should be shot with Sharman's head on Boman's stomach to show the affection between father and son. I loved the idea so much that I shifted the shot to another room and it took a couple of more hours, but I went ahead with that suggestion.

Nirmal: *Till now, you have been loyal to Sanjay Suri, Juhi Chawla and your brand of people. You have your own camp, Onir camp, if I may call them. It would be easier for you because they know your mind. Tomorrow if you enter the star system, would you be able to control your film?*

Onir: I will not work with people who don't understand my kind of filmmaking.

Nirmal: *Will you not want to make typical masala films?*

Onir: No, I don't see myself making those films. I want to make a certain kind of film that I believe in. I did have the opportunity. After *My Brother Nikhil*, a big production house wanted me to work with them, but I was very clear that I didn't identify with those films. I have nothing against it, but I will be making disasters if I even try.

Nirmal: *You don't want to make a* Dilwale Dulhania Le Jayenge, *Yash Chopra kind of film.*

Onir: I won't be able to because I don't have the skills.

Nirmal: *But with* Sorry Bhai, *you were trying to go closer to the mainstream.*

Onir: That's as close as I can get to mainstream filmmaking. If you do a romance, it'll be in that space. It won't be all pretty where everybody's nice. Many will be shocked at the way a girl talks, but come on, women talk like that. In India, women are bereft of any sexuality. So when she says, 'Main use pata ke dikhaongi, aur uski Maa ko bhi pata loongi' a lot of people will go 'Oh my God!' But for me, that's why I love this woman. I have seen my women friends. They do so much of scheming and talk about sex, much more than men do. But in Indian films, you just bereft them of all this. Again, the lovemaking scene in the store, people are shocked by it.

Nirmal: *Coming back to* I Am, *you have funded this film through crowd funding. How did the idea come about?*

Onir: The idea came from necessity. I wanted to make them as separate feature films. Again, financing was a problem and Sanjay Suri, my business partner, came up with the idea that instead of sitting and sulking, I should write them as short stories. He reminded me that just like four or five years ago I had made *My Brother Nikhil* and I wasn't scared, after four films I should not be afraid and nothing should stop me to get separate finance for each. So then I started writing them as short stories, but linking them in a way where they could be shown as one feature film because

Courtesy: Onir.

in India, you don't have a market for short films as such. At the same time, I knew that if the finance didn't come, one could stop at any time. It was shot very carefully. Then while writing, an idea came to me. A lot of people keep messaging me on Facebook, on Twitter wanting to know more about films, wanting to get connected, but very scared because there's no transparency. So I thought I would just put up a post on my Facebook account saying that this is what I want to do, so if you want to be a part of it, you can either volunteer to work for me, or you can give ₹1,000 and you can become a co-owner, or give a lakh and become a co-producer. So the first cheque came in after three days from a student in Pune who sent ₹1,500, his/her pocket money. This person sent it because he/she had been abused for six years and felt that with this film he/she would be liberated and get a voice. For me, I knew the film would happen the minute I got ₹1,500. We raised nearly 10 million through Facebook and Twitter, and it was the first film throughout South Asia that was done through social networking, crowd funding and crowd sourcing. We did both, as in raise money and talent.

Preeti: *In fact, this brings me to my next question which is, how do you think digitization in general and social networking in particular will impact the dynamics of the industry?*

Onir: It is already kind of there, if you really look at Pay-for-TV or Direct-to-Home. Increasingly, a lot of people are watching films at home or on the mobile. When TV initially came, people thought films would be wiped out. But come what may, if you sit and watch a film in a theatre, it is a collective experience. It can never be replaced. I think it's a question of economics; the price of tickets came down and it was reasonable. Today, if I want to watch a film, I would love to go with a group of friends to a theatre. It's very different from sitting at home with five people and watching a DVD. The group experience is not there. You will have all forms of cinema and also different forms for different media because if you're watching *Sholay* on your mobile, you won't get it. They will start making content that works on mobile. What social networking is going to do is open up huge avenues for independent filmmaking not only to make your film, but also to build an audience. You, as a filmmaker, can create and interact with your audience. If you don't have the money for television publicity and paying mainstream newspapers who won't write about you unless you pay, then there is the internet for you.

You can reach out to people, sell your DVDs and do so much. It is going to become an important tool because increasingly, the audience that I would like to reach out to, are not watching television, but sitting on the internet. I can reach them much faster through Facebook or Twitter than if I put up a 6-million ad on television.

Nirmal: Has crowd funding come to stay?

Onir: I think so. Even for my future projects, I will partly raise money through crowd funding.

Preeti: How does this really work? If somebody funds your project, do they get a share of your profits?

Onir: There are different ways. Abroad there are platforms like Indiegogo or Kickstarter that raise money. These are purely contributions because people like to be a part of good cinema and support causes. In India, there is no such platform. Actually, very soon a platform is starting, and my next film is going to be the first film which that platform is going to put up.

There are various modules. You give certain merchandise for a certain contribution, credits, and then above a certain amount you give a profit cheque. So it depends on the various slabs and you work on that.

Nirmal: In I Am, there is a part where you have Juhi Chawla and Manisha Koirala. I am yet to see a more powerful film on Kashmir. There is no victor and everyone is a loser. Everyone is defeated in the end.

Also, in this film, female narration is dominant. Are you wilfully trying to exclude the stories of men from this part?

Onir: I think, for me the story of Megha was very important. For me, war is mostly created by men. Even in Kashmir, women don't play a big role in decision-making. They are only, eternally, losing their fathers, sons, brothers and lovers. They are not so much an active part. They join in later because they are losing loved ones, but decisions are made for them and they are told what to do. I am not directly talking about the political conflict in Kashmir, but I set it up as the backdrop. It is so complex, and in a short story how do you do it? I thought I would show it from the perspective of two women. Who are always the worst hit in any situation of conflict? Both of these women are brought up together. One has lost her home, her identity and become a refugee but moved on in life because she's left the valley, though not out of choice. The other who has stayed on has a home, family, but is stagnating. You look at Manisha, right from her hair; the look that I wanted was of someone who is struggling. Both these women are in their forties and single because they are struggling to just survive.

Nirmal: *Why Kashmir?*

Onir: Kashmir, for two reasons. I, myself, am a kind of a refugee, so I identify with being homeless. My parents were refugees from Bangladesh. They came to Bhutan, where I was born and brought up. In the nineties, because of political problems in Bhutan, we had to leave again even though we were unhappy. For me, that was a home to which I couldn't go back. My most precious memories, but I couldn't go back.

I had gone to Kashmir while researching another story and came across all these deserted houses. I also knew the story of my friend Sanjay Suri, whose father was shot dead and they had to leave overnight. When I was doing research, Sanjay went back to Kashmir after 17 years. When he went to his house, he couldn't even enter because it was so traumatic. Also, after talking to a lot of young Kashmiris,

I became aware that be it our government or anyone else, there has been no effort in our education system to make the younger generation aware that there's a huge population of refugees. For them, it's that they have run away and are leading better lives in the US. That's why there is a dialogue that says, '*Bhag gaya ya bhagaya gaya?*' There is a difference. Did they leave or were they forced to leave? There is this erasing of history. Today a 17-year-old Kashmiri boy has never had a Hindu Pandit friend. That was such an integral part of Kashmiri society. It troubled me that 300,000 people who were part of a community left, and there is so much of silence. Be it in cinema, be it in the government, there is silence.

Today if you go to Kashmir (and I'm all for freedom, I'm not for oppression), if I were a Kashmiri I would hate the Indian army. Kashmiri women are so beautiful, but the look these army men have... you don't want to be there. At the same time these guys, they come from Bihar, from somewhere, they know that they might die anytime and people hate them. It's a very difficult situation, but the Government of India has its corrupt officials, army guys leading a fabulous life, whereas the normal soldiers lead miserable lives. The quarters they stay in are dirty, filthy, whereas the senior guys stay in lavish bungalows. Some of them would come to the sets and there would always be these young Kashmiri girls with them. Then you realize that their fathers or brothers were in prison and these girls were being exploited. It is so messed up. Our government has done nothing to make these parts inclusive. Though, again, I'm all for human rights, for the freedom of people, but not freedom which excludes people of other religions, gender and sexuality.

For me, a Kashmir without Kashmiri Pandits is as dangerous as thinking of Hindu Indians suddenly saying that all Muslims should go out. It's the same thing, and anything that divides people using religion is a very dangerous thing. In Kashmir, the women have always been far more energetic, intelligent and progressive than the Kashmiri men; you talk to the women and you realize, but with the militants coming in, the first thing that happened to them was covering up; their schools were burnt down.

So what is freedom? You are talking about freedom when you are throwing out people of other religious communities. Not giving women their freedom — who are you to decide all this? So for me, this film was more of a dialogue because what we miss in our country is dialogue. Unless you talk about things, you will never begin to question. I was pleasantly surprised at the amount of Kashmiri Muslims who joined in financially for this film apart from a lot of Pandits, and who were very open to receiving the film. I feel that the problem with our government is that it is not willing to talk, to say 'Yes, we're sorry. We messed up.' They are busy going to these idiotic golf courses, while, on the contrary, the best hospital's condition is such that one of my producers (his grandmother had to have an operation) was getting late for the shoot because he was at the medical shop buying thread and calling up the hospital to enquire about the thickness of the thread... imagine. So what are we talking about — having a Taj hotel there, a golf course, when the basics are not there? At the same time, for a lot of rich Kashmiris, despite all the complaints, so much of money that is being pumped into the state. When they are complaining about life, they should see the way 73% of Bombay lives in slums. That's a miserable life. They don't have proper food or fresh air. But at the same time if you really think, this situation of conflict suits so many people. The war economics is working well for them. For the Kashmiri men as well, it suits them perfectly with their big houses. In the evening, they go out to play badminton, socialize whenever they want, travel across the world outside India and lead double lives. While their beautiful women, sitting at home as their wives, take care of their food and kids. Why would they want anything to change? It's again the women, who are just not being able to break free.

You will not see so many Kashmiri girls studying in other colleges or coming for modelling, even though they are as beautiful. It is only the Kashmiri men who have all the possibilities opening up for them.

Nirmal: *Do you see the possibility of making a full-blown movie on Kashmir?*

Onir: I had gone there for research on a film script that I am working on. It is a political thriller.

Nirmal: *One question that had to come up is that are you trying to promote and get space for alternative sexuality?*

Onir: 'Promote' is the wrong word. It's not an advertisement that you need to promote. I am a strong believer in human rights that includes gender, sexuality or religious minorities. I think the best example of that is *I Am* where it is talking of women's rights, religious divide, child abuse, which is across sexuality and it talks of sexuality. So it talks of all kinds of minorities. For me, it's been an extremely important fact, for example, all my films have very strong women characters. So representation of women, minus being defined by their male counterparts, is extremely important.

It's not 'My Sister Anu' at the end of the day, it's 'My Brother Nikhil'. It's almost like the definition is attached... Even in *Sorry Bhai*, the central protagonist, the driving protagonist, is not the guy. It's the girl who always says 'no' to the elder brother. She is the one who tells him; the guy does not have the balls. She is the one who says *Main use pata ke rahoongi*. Even Shabana is the driving force, and that is extremely important for me.

Secondly, as a gay person in a society where you are still criminalized by the law, it is extremely important for me to use the tool of my cinema (unlike a lot of filmmakers who belong to the LGBT community, who don't use the medium for whatever reason) to talk about everything that troubles me as a human being. I am not a politician, I am not a social worker, but I can use the tool of my cinema, whichever format it is, to communicate, to spread awareness and advocate acceptance.

Preeti: *In I Am, why does the character of Rahul Bose, the MD of a multinational, succumb to the pressure from an ordinary policeman? Why couldn't we show something else?*

Onir: Because if you do a little research, you will realize how many gay men go through that all the time, who are by their identity criminalized by the law. That is why this film is supported by 'Humsafar Trust' and 'Naz Foundation' that are basically the ones responsible for the Delhi High Court changing the law. They were the lawyers of 'Naz'. One of the reasons why they majorly support this film (of course they provided me with the research material for that story) is that there is a huge percentage.... recently, I think about two months back, it was in the newspaper that there was a gay party happening at Madh Island. The police came in and 400 men were arrested and brought into jail, made to kneel down and hold their ears. They were told to give ₹1,400 each. They were all managing directors of big corporates, some of them I know. When these men asked the police why they had to pay this amount, they were slapped. It happens all the time.

Preeti: *When you say criminalized by law, what do you mean?*

Onir: It means that you can be imprisoned for life, or there is some huge fine if you are caught in a homosexual act. Therefore, by definition, in India you don't have the right till now, except for Delhi jurisdiction, which happened two years ago, the constitutional right. It is unlike in Nepal, where it is legalized. So when you are legally empowered, you can do much more. You can fight people if you are legal. It's like going to Iran and saying, 'Why can't you fight?' You will just be beheaded if you are a gay person. Though, again, in a lot of these countries you have a huge section of the population that is from the gay community.

Nirmal: *Do you think that had you been making movies on mainstream themes also, instead of* My Brother Nikhil *and* I Am, *funding would have been easier for you, considering the way the Mumbai film industry works?*

Onir: It's a question that's totally irrelevant for me because there is no question of choice. It's like saying that today if you become heterosexual, you will be accepted.

Nirmal: *As good or as bad as that?*

Onir: Yes. I'm not someone who likes to live a life of pretention and just like I am open about my identity, despite the difficulties. Similarly, I'll make the films that I want to and not what the market wants me to.

Nirmal: *One more question about crowd funding. Is it better to have one* paan-*chewing* lalaji *giving you crores of money than having 400 or 500 people funding you, considering the* lalaji knows nothing about filmmaking and will give you a lot of freedom?

Onir: Most *lalajis*, and if he is a *paan*-chewing one, will definitely say, 'Accha isko le lo film mein' or 'Accha meri iske saath photo khichwa do' and much more. That's the danger. If you are passionate about films, you want to work with people who are equally passionate and that energy of 400 people is much more, and that is all positive energy. That's much more precious because there is someone who understands what you are doing.

Nirmal: *How do you rate/slot yourself — as an art filmmaker or as a new wave Indian filmmaker?*

Onir: I see myself as a new wave contemporary Indian filmmaker.

Nirmal: *People like you, Dibakar, Neeraj Pandey… has the new wave cinema come full circle, come to stay here?*

Onir: Yes, I think we have come to stay here. There's been a huge gap in between. You had Shyam Benegal, Ketan Mehta, Adoor Gopalakrishnan and then there was an entire vacuum, and I think now again is an exciting time where you have different forms of not-so-mainstream cinema, be it Dibakar or Anurag.

Nirmal: *But the best thing is that now you have cheaper technology available to you.*

Onir: I think the entire digital revolution is throwing open something, but at the same time what is difficult now is that, unlike in Europe or America, where you have a very strong exhibition system, where parallel cinema…. The idea of parallel cinema is that it is word-of-mouth cinema. But today when you are releasing your film, you release with a big film like *Ra One*, but unless your film performs in the first three days, you are shifted to afternoon shows or morning shows. Your film is meant for a mature audience. Now who is not going to go to office, and come and watch your movie? They'll say, 'I will see it on TV'. So the entire system of exhibition kills independent cinema. You know, when it started we all thought, *'Five screens hain, chalo ek screen to hamare liye hai'*, but it is not there for us. The whole idea that the multiplexes were created to support different forms of cinema has been killed because today if there is a big film, all the screens will be given to the big film and all the best timings will be given to the big film. It is all about studios, power and the exhibition system in this country suck.

Our government does nothing. Today they'll make it tax-free, after six weeks, when your film is already gone plus with each state, it is separate. So firstly cinema, unfortunately, in our country is not treated as an art form. I think that cinema can play such a strong role in society, which is not being given its place. Today the taxation, the exhibition system and the third big challenge, which is part of the exhibition system is ticketing. When you go to see *Ra One*, a ₹300 ticket, 1,500-million film and you go to see *I Am*, ₹300 ticket, 15-million film.... why? You will not, as a buyer, pay the same when you are buying something made in gold and something which is made with something else. The economics are different. Today if *I Am* was also shown in the same theatre for ₹50, a student would see *Ra One* and then say, *'Chalo ye pachas rupay ka hai, ye bhi dekh lete hain'*. I don't need ₹300, for me ₹50 is enough because my budget is so small. And I think that is a big deterrent for independent filmmakers who are making small-budget films.

The third thing is publicity. Again, today, some leading newspapers, especially like 'Times'.... your film might be getting awards, might be a good film, but they will not write one line about your film unless you pay. Media, which is supposed to support good cinema, has become a mere advertorial. So not only do they read articles, but a certain rating also comes with that money. So people are pushed to watch rubbish. At the same time, it is difficult to make them aware of something that does not have the budget because for my kind of a film, a support system is not there. While the media will go on that Indian cinema must change, they do nothing. So the support system for independent cinema is extremely small. The good thing is that the National Film Development Corporation is once again looking into the structure and things will change. I feel that not only as a country do we need a chain of Indian cinema spaces to show these kinds of films, but also to make available films from other states. How will we grow as a nation unless as a cinema-going audience we watch Bengali films, Marathi films, Tamil films... we have such amazing films. Why are we bothered about overseas? We should cross over within our own country and we'll have enough audience, we don't need the world. If the entire South started watching our films and we started watching their films, wow! Imagine the kind of revenue that would happen within the country. But again our government does nothing to bridge the gaps that are within our country.

There is so much of divide—north–south, east–west. Everywhere it's divided.

Preeti: *As a student of comparative literature, how do you compare the themes that are being dealt with in Indian writing vis-à-vis the sort of subjects that are being dealt with in Indian cinema?*

Onir: I think Indian literature, like Indian films, is also going through a lot of change. It's a very difficult phase because we have become such a money-driven society. Today, we are more interested in our children learning

Bollywood dancing so that they can go to a reality show and earn money than making them learn our own classical dance forms. Our best teachers are sitting in Germany teaching classical Indian music and dance there. Similarly, even in terms of literature, we have started valuing pulp writers more than an Amitava Ghosh. So today, a critic for films will proudly say that in the end what matters is entertainment, entertainment, entertainment, but they forget that brainless entertainment is harmful to the society. When you say leave your brains at home and come and just enjoy the film, it doesn't mean anything. Every film has a message. Mostly these films have very regressive messages towards gender, towards sexuality, towards religion, where everyone is caricatured and one makes fun of the other. Everything is North India or Gujrati-centric, where the money is, where Raj is always good. So I feel that the same thing is happening everywhere. Today, good writers face a lot of problems, and I really feel in a vast country like ours, there is no dearth of stories. I wish there was much more interaction between our novelists and our filmmakers, more exchange, adaptation etc., but somehow it is not happening.

Nirmal: *Most of you sensitive filmmakers have not taken up good literature for filmmaking.*

Onir: I don't think that is necessary because if you have your own stories to tell, like especially most independent filmmakers are writers–directors. They write their own films. They want to tell their own story. At the same time, I'll give you an example, for the last one year I have desperately been trying to get in touch with a Pakistani writer set in London, called Nadeem Aslam. I haven't got a reply and it becomes so difficult. Because if you are an independent filmmaker, your budgets are small, some of them think we need huge money to buy rights. So today, we buy the rights of *The Reluctant Fundamentalist*, but I can't. I would like to do *The Hungry Tide*, but I don't have the kind of money to even take the initial rights, to even let me try to get finance because you have to make a certain payment. So it is not easy for independent filmmakers, but people are slowly looking at literature. But the joke is that a lot of them are thinking, 'Let's look at making, not only remakes of foreign films with rights, but also foreign literature, not so much of Indian.'

Tigmanshu Dhulia

Source: Authors.

Born into the splendour of mellow Allahabadi culture, filmmaker Tigmanshu Dhulia was no stranger to literary luminaries and progressive intellectuals. With a mother who was a professor of Sanskrit and a father who practised law at the High Court, Tigmanshu, the youngest of three sons, was nonetheless quick to reject academics in favour of the performing arts. The solemnity of a steady government job was unappealing to him, and it was not long before Tigmanshu realized his true calling.

Dhulia went to school at St. Joseph's College and Anglo Bengali Intermediate College. During the final two years of school, he became an active member of the University's film club. It was here that Dhulia was introduced to the wonders of the French new wave and Italian neo-realism. While pursuing his Bachelor's degree from Allahabad University, Tigmanshu was continually immersed in theatre, music and student politics. In search of a liberal artistic environment, he joined NSD, New Delhi in 1986 but remained disillusioned with the insular and unexciting character of the institute.

Dhulia's first project was as an assistant for Pradip Kishen's *Electric Moon*. He then went on to adapt short stories for a television show on Doordarshan. But the real break in his career came with Shekhar Kapur's *Bandit Queen*. Dhulia was the casting director, but ended up writing the dialogue for the film as well. After this brief stint with the world of Hindi cinema, he went back to television and directed popular shows like *Just Mohabbat* and *Naya Daur*.

Haasil (2003), starring Jimmy Shergill and Hrishita Bhatt, was Tigmanshu's first piece of cinema based on student politics set in Allahabad, Uttar Pradesh. It revolves around the two young lovers who are caught in an endless chain of power games. The film was hailed for its honesty and hard-hitting depiction of murky campus wars.

Next came *Charas: A Joint Effort* (2004), which dealt with the seedy ongoings in the drug-racketeering business. Replete with songs and subplots, Dhulia had established himself as a director who was unafraid of making potboilers that were simultaneously riveting. His third film *Shagird* (2011), a ruthless action thriller starring Nana Patekar, though subject to mixed reviews, was proof that this mainstream filmmaker with a penchant for compelling frames and stories was here to stay.

By now, it was clear that Dhulia was a master of his craft, in complete control of each scene and that the story would remain king in all his films. The *Saheb, Biwi Aur Gangster* series is an example of his unique form of filmmaking where the lines of popular and aesthetic cinema begin to blur. A modern remake of the old Guru Dutt classic *Saheb, Bibi Aur Ghulam* (1962), (mischievously renamed *Saheb, Biwi Aur Gangster* or *The Master, the Wife and the Gangster*) it was a bold and modern interpretation of the original. A sensuous and refreshingly new tale of the decaying aristocracy of Uttar Pradesh, at no point did Dhulia let on that this was an old story being retold.

Saheb, Biwi Aur Gangster (2011) and its sequel *Saheb, Biwi Aur Gangster Returns* (2013) are layered portrayals of human desire, ambition and personal inadequacies contextualized within the landscape of a decadent royalty coming to terms with the new powers of modern politics. Both were critically acclaimed films that marked Tigmanshu as a filmmaker with his own brand of earthy cinema for a contemporary audience.

Wedged between the two aforementioned was Dhulia's *Paan Singh Tomar* (2012), a biopic on the sportsman-turned-dacoit who was failed by his own government. Touted as a moving and powerful depiction of neglected heroes of the nation, the film performed exceedingly well and received the National Film Award for the Best Feature Film. The film, devoid of stars, (Irrfan Khan played Tomar) was convincingly lapped up by the audience—a sign that Dhulia has arrived.

Dhulia is undeterred by narrow definitions of cinema that slot films as either *masala* fare or alternative. The bottom line for him is that a film must entertain the viewer, no matter what.

The Alternative as Mainstream—Blurring the Boundaries in Cinematic Tradition

Nirmal: *What does Tigmanshu mean?*

Tigmanshu: It means the sun, actually, the slanting rays of the sun. One who has not yet risen fully (laughs).

Nirmal: *You belong to Uttarakhand. Your grandfather was a freedom fighter. But where did you grow up?*

Tigmanshu: I was in Allahabad till my graduation.

Preeti: *Tell us something about your growing years in Allahabad.*

Tigmanshu: Apart from my parents, I have two elder brothers. My father was in the judiciary and he had to come to the High Court, so we were in Allahabad. My mother was a professor of Sanskrit. My parents were quite liberal. Our home usually had a studious atmosphere. My father had studied at Allahabad University under people like Firaq Gorakhpuri and Harivansh Rai Bachchan. After the breakup of the Communist Party, he was the Secretary of SFI, Uttar Pradesh, so people like Amrit Rai used to come to our house. In that sense, I have been very lucky.

My parents enjoyed watching films. They watched mainstream movies as well as films by directors like Shyam Benegal. They would always take me along, but if there was an adult film then they would be in a quandary. I would throw tantrums. But if I did not enjoy a film then too I would get upset. I never liked 'social' films. There was a film called *Anurag* and I was so angry because I did not enjoy it. I have seen many films with my father.

Allahabad, as a town, is a beautiful and seamless blend of Indian and Western philosophies, and that too, without any pretence. There was no 'Yo man!' sort of scene in this town. For example, Amar Singh *sahib*, at the university, would come on a cycle chewing betel leaf and dressed in a *dhoti* with a *tilak* on his forehead, but spoke and taught us immaculate English. My brother played the guitar. I had a rock band. The music scene in Allahabad was quite evolved.

I was not interested in academics and did not perform well in the ICSE Board. As a matter of fact, I failed in class 10. The experience of failing a class, hiding from classmates and blaming the world for what was one's own mistake was an unpleasant one. After the exams, we went to my maternal grandparents in Dehradun and discovered that the Punjab School Board held the board examinations twice a year. My father asked me to stay on in Dehradun, study hard and pass the exams. I got admission in a school called Ideal School (laughs). The principal of the school instructed me to take tuitions. I was expected to learn *Gurmukhi*, which was difficult because in class 10 it was at an advanced level. The subjects were difficult. We heard that, apparently, no one in the history of the school had cleared the exam in the last six months. Most took at least a year or more. So, basically, the institute was a money-making outfit.

Somehow, I was able to clear the 10th Board exams in six months (with just 58%). Surprisingly, it was during that phase in my life that I watched many films. I watched a film every day. My neighbour and friend, Taranjeet, and I would finish dinner and run to catch the show at eight. I was exposed to old Hindi cinema that I had not seen with my parents, for example, Rajendra Kumar's films.

I returned to Allahabad for my 11th standard. That is when I got involved in university activities, such as the film club in Sachin Tiwari *ji*'s theatre, and also in political activity. My elder brothers influenced everything that I did. They were part of all these activities and I imitated them. I ended up in this line of work, whereas they pursued other things.

At that time Allahabad was a town that was culturally alive in every way. Be it music, theatre or films. I saw films like *The Godfather*, *All the President's Men* and *For Whom the Bell Tolls* in a movie hall. My Applied Physics professor, Professor Chattopadhay, would have 16 mm prints of films brought down from the National Film Archive in Pune. I would watch directors like Godard or Truffaut and not understand anything, but I was affected by the images in those films and they were imprinted in my psyche. At that time, I did not have any background understanding of the French new wave or Italian neo-realism. It was only later that I comprehended this kind of cinema.

Actually, I am a cocktail of commercial Hindi cinema and intellectual cinema. I feel there should be the presence of both in my films. A film has to be entertaining. Filmmaking is not like writing poetry. It is not for a select audience. Also, a lot of money is involved. Many people are involved in the making of a film. It should reach the masses, at whatever level it can. At the same time, it should have a profound layer that satisfies you as a filmmaker.

Nirmal: *The story is king in your films. All your stories are very powerful. Where does this aptitude for storytelling come from?*

Tigmanshu: Maybe this is the influence of my theatre training. I do not have a very technical understanding of films, which in a way is good. My training dictates that content will decide the form.

Nirmal: *Do you feel that formal training, for example, a course in film studies, hampers the freedom of a director and limits their vision? Do you feel that because you were not trained there was a greater freedom to make films that you felt like making?*

Tigmanshu: Some films are such that they become reference points in your life. Let me give you an example. There is something called a point-of-view shot where the camera is moving but there is no subject. You know that somebody's eyes are watching the scene — there is a reference. Similarly, there are certain filmmakers, who become a point of reference for your filmmaking (it becomes the grammar of your film) and you cannot make your film without utilizing their art and technique. *Battleship Potemkin's* editing style set a benchmark for all films to follow, and now, ad-filmmakers use that style extensively. Having said that I feel that some filmmakers are a product of cinema, whereas I am a product of life. Quentin Tarantino is a great filmmaker, but I think he will always remain a product of cinema. Directors like Francis Ford Coppola and Martin Scorcese are products of life, which is always better.

Nirmal: *Tell us a little about your political activities during your college years. Were you volatile?*

Tigmanshu: I was not very volatile. I was a part of the Progressive Students' Organization, but mostly involved with their cultural wing. Of course, there were times when we too would go to places like Gorakhpur where Left-wing activities were in operation. We would make posters, perform *nukkad natak* (street plays) and sing songs.

Preeti: *Was Jimmy Shergill's character, Aniruddha, in* Haasil *(2003) slightly autobiographical?*

Tigmanshu: Yes. A bit.

Preeti: *So were you more involved in the arts and cultural side of the organization rather than outright political propaganda? Did you ever aspire to join politics?*

Tigmanshu: At that point of time the aspiration was not there, but now I sometimes feel that eventually one should join politics.

Preeti: *The chain of events that you portrayed in a movie like* Haasil *showed the dark side of student politics. Do you feel that there was any constructive politics in Allahabad University (or any other educational institution)? Or was it a self-serving practice?*

Tigmanshu: If you belong to a party that teaches you something in your formative years, even if it just introduces you to good books then it is all right. But there are cases where it becomes ugly. There was an incident in Ujjain, Madhya Pradesh, where students had killed a professor.

Preeti: *Tell us about your days at NSD. What influenced you and what was your social circle like? Also, was it a dramatic shift from Allahabad?*

Tigmanshu: Well, there was a lot happening in Allahabad and I was happy. The theatre was good, the music scene was good, and so were the films. In your own town, people know you and you are somewhat of a hero playing the guitar. The girls like you. But there is always a tendency to want more.

A new train called Prayag Raj Express was introduced between Allahabad and New Delhi. It changed Allahabad completely. Before that a train trip to Delhi was a momentous event. In a way, it destroyed Allahabad. Allahabad was a town of lawyers and of eminent judges with their colonial houses and big cars. There was a tradition where the sons of these judges would follow them in their profession. But with the train, people started sending their kids to Delhi University. Their children went away to practice law in the High Court and Supreme Court in Delhi. People started their own businesses by getting goods from Delhi and selling them here. So in a way, the so-called 'cream' of Allahabad and its old-world feel disappeared. Then the emergence of regional politics made the whole atmosphere of Allahabad just rotten.

Nirmal: *How did your family react to your joining NSD?*

Tigmanshu: My father had already passed away when I joined the university. My mother was there. There was really no objection of any kind from anyone in the family. My brothers have always been very supportive. My mother used to think that I would not do anything in life. As a matter of fact, I even trained in stenography in the hope that when one of my elder brothers would become a lawyer, I would at least get hired as a *munshi*.

Even while I was doing the course at NSD, my mother kept suggesting that I do a correspondence course in law. But she never objected to my choice of subject. By that time, one of my brothers had joined the navy and the other had begun practising law.

Preeti: *So you belong to a privileged family.*

Tigmanshu: Yes. The first Maruti 800 in Allahabad was in our house.

Nirmal: *Tell us about your experience at NSD.*

Tigmanshu: Before joining NSD, I had gone to check it out. It was not as if I was hell-bent on going there or doing theatre. I wanted to go to any institute that had a relatively liberal and intellectually stimulating atmosphere. I had given the exam for FTI as well. When I had gone to NSD to check it out, there was a play being performed, Prasanna *ji*'s *Fujiyama*. I was impressed with the play. Then I saw that girls were smoking cigarettes and everyone was drinking tea together, even at 10 in the night. Also, there were no vagabonds there. So I decided that I wanted to join NSD. It was not so much for the theatre, but because it had a permissive ambience. I do not deny it was very exciting to see and meet the big names in theatre, but within the next six months my illusion of this grandeur was shattered. The kind of theatre that was being performed at NSD would never become popular. There would be four people in the audience. There would be some claps. Nothing more.

Nirmal: *A very niche crowd comes to watch these plays and only they understand the nuanced performances. Do you feel a city like Delhi is ready for this kind of theatre?*

Tigmanshu: Well, when you compare theatre in Mumbai to that in Delhi then the latter is far better. Though Marathi theatre in Mumbai is good, the most popular form of theatre there is predominantly Gujarati theatre where people like you and me cannot enjoy ourselves. The dialogues are cheap, mobile phones are ringing, there are shrieking children and of course, tea and popcorn. But they have packed houses and expensive tickets.

Preeti: *Has your learning at NSD influenced your filmmaking?*

Tigmanshu: To be honest, I did not really enjoy my time at NSD. I was either in the library reading books or somewhere drinking tea. I watched many films at Shakuntalam theatre for ₹5. Then I would also frequent the Russian Centre of Science and Culture and the Japanese Cultural Centre.

Preeti: *Why were you disappointed with NSD?*

Tigmanshu: After getting out of NSD in 1990, I did one or two plays. A classmate of mine had directed a play and the show was in Jammu. You would not believe it, but between 1990 and 2012 I have just seen one or two plays. I get very bored. I do not enjoy myself. But this is my personal opinion, and I am not saying that the plays are bad. In all probability, I am at fault. For example, Naseer bhai's (Naseeruddin Shah) *Ismat Apa Ke Naam* was a play that received great reviews and people asked me to go watch it. But I never went.

What I fail to understand is the fact that NSD does not admit good-looking students, especially girls. In the garb of theatre, they are continuously destroying people's lives. Invariably, all these students from NSD come to Mumbai in hopes of making it big. Since I am a senior, I often meet many of the pass outs and I know for a fact that they really struggle in Mumbai. At least I offer them tea and food even if there is no guarantee of work, but they are not even allowed to enter in any of the other offices. It is no one's fault except the NSD because it produces unrealistic hope in these people. Why does the institute provide admission to such students? They can never become heroes. Even a great actor like Naseeruddin Shah was never able to become one.

There was a girl in my class, Navneet Nishan, who later starred in the famous Hindi soap opera, *Tara*; then she was a sex bomb. When she stepped out, everyone's ideology would go for a toss (laughs).

Preeti: *Did you come to Mumbai immediately after completing your course at NSD?*

Tigmanshu: No. For four years after that I stayed in Delhi. I used to live in Mayur Vihar. I was quite fortunate that I was associated with films even in Delhi. For once, I had decided that I did not want to act. I had played the role of the central character in a play directed by Bhanu Bharti. It was Ibsen's *The Wild Duck*, a difficult play. He used to cast the play on the basis of readings. I read it with ease and ended up playing the main role. But he never guided us in any way. The translation of the play was by Yashpal *ji* who was very good, but this particular one was bad. The language was so clichéd, whereas the play was a realistic one. I did not know how to go about this play, and there was no guidance and no focus. I was the youngest in my class. I was 22 when I passed out. On top of that, it turned out to be a costly play.

I remember I was dreading the performance and hoped that somehow the play would be cancelled. I could see that people were leaving the show. There were just three or four people left. It was such a flop. What brought it down was the translation. For example, Amrit Rai *ji*'s translation of Shakespeare's *Hamlet* into Hindi is effortless and thoroughly enjoyable. So then I started translating plays and I decided that I did not want to act.

Fortunately, after I passed out of NSD, Ketan Mehta's *Sardar* (1993) was being made. Now there was a professor, Robin Das, who was teaching design and direction at NSD. He was a favourite with the students because he would take classes at the teashop and allowed smoking during class. He was also the kind of man who would go through periods of drinking and then abstinence. Ketan Mehta approached him to undertake the art direction for *Sardar*.

So one fine day, Robin Das asked me to assist him and I was more than glad to do so.

It was a different matter that I had no knowledge in art direction; I could not even draw a straight line. I would always be the worst student in carpentry class or make-up class. So you can imagine. But I understood that a lot of research was required to pull off design in this film. I would spend many hours at the libraries at Teen Murti Bhavan and JNU, and conduct my research. It was a great experience. Unfortunately, when the film started production, Robin Das went on a drinking spree. There was a 16-day schedule in Mardoli, Gujarat and that is where a fight broke out between Ketan and Robin *da*.

Even though there were problems in our department, Ketan realized that I was a hard-working lad. I had not slept a wink during those 16 days. Eventually, Ketan removed Robin *da*. While paying us, Robin *da* decided not to pay me there and told me that he would settle my dues in Delhi. I was a young boy of 23 who had got recently married and wanted to go back home, so I began to cry. I remember clearly that the Filmfare Awards was showing on TV when I went to Ketan still crying and told him that Robin had refused to pay me. So Ketan took a stand and in front of everyone demanded that he pay me my due. I was very happy and went back home.

It so happened that filmmaker Pradip Kishen was making his film, *Electric Moon*, so I went to his home at Malcha Marg and asked to assist him. He agreed to keep me for a 10-day trial period, and finally I was there for the whole movie. The producer of this film was Bobby Bedi who took me on his next project. That was the year of the girl child. Farrukh Dhondy commissioned Bobby Bedi to make a six-part series called *Krishna's Dream* based on short stories by Indian women writers. This was for UK's Channel 4. Bobby Bedi commissioned this series for Doordarshan as well. I adapted all six stories for the series and independently directed one of the stories.

Bobby Bedi was also the producer of *Bandit Queen* and told me that I would be the casting director for the film. So I got involved with that as well. Shekhar Kapur was carrying photos of Dimple Kapadia, Mita Vashist and others; all of them with a red band tied around their foreheads. On my green-coloured Chetak scooter, I took Shekhar *ji* around Mandi House looking for actors. Ranjeet Kapoor was writing the dialogues for the film. He had a habit of taking on work but never completing it. He wrote the first 20 odd scenes of *Bandit Queen* and then disappeared. So then Shekhar *ji* asked me to write the dialogues. In the process, I began to handle multiple things on the set. After the shooting wrapped up, he asked me whether I would come to Bombay to assist him. That is when I came to Mumbai.

Nirmal: *What was it like working on a film like* Bandit Queen? *Did you ever think that it would receive the kind of critical acclaim that it did?*

Tigmanshu: No. But *Bandit Queen* was a life-altering experience. I would put it in the same category as one's birth, one's marriage and one's first child. It was that defining moment in my life when I stood on my own two feet.

Artistically, it was very satisfying to work on *Bandit Queen* because I knew I was contributing to the film in a major way. You see, usually, the work of an AD is to run around and organize. It is not really a creative job, except maybe in setting up the background action for a scene. I did that and learnt a lot from it. Apart from that I was doing dialogue and casting.

I must tell you the role that this movie played in changing the face of Hindi cinema. Owing to *Bandit Queen*, there was a kind of exodus from Delhi. The whole of Mandi

House was empty after *Bandit Queen*. The cream of actors in Delhi migrated to Mumbai. Be it Saurabh Shukla, Manoj Bajpai, Seema Biswas, Raghuvir Yadav—all came to Mumbai. Before *Bandit Queen,* there were very few theatre actors from Delhi who would come to Mumbai.

Nirmal: *The label of NSD must have helped you.*

Tigmanshu: Yes, it did. For example, if today I have to make a film in Manipur or Trivandrum, I have friends there and can tap local talent. The non-Hindi speaking students from NSD mostly go into regional theatre, and sometimes into regional cinema. So I will always have friends across the country.

Preeti: *Initially, you were working as an AD. Were you not impatient to earn more as you were already married and living in a city like Mumbai?*

Tigmanshu: I have been fortunate because my elder brother who is in the navy was also in Mumbai at that time. He was posted in Indian Naval Ship (INS) Hamla. He had a big house, and he asked me to come and stay with him. For a year, my wife and I stayed with my brother. Actually, my wife and my *bhabhi* (elder brother's wife) are also childhood friends. They have a very good equation with each other.

While working with Shekhar *ji* I earned a small amount, barely ₹250, that too only on days of shooting, but it was worth it because I was the assistant of a star director. Then Shekhar *ji* was made the creative head of a new channel called BI TV. He asked Saurabh Shukla and me to produce a serial for this channel. So, the two of us opened a company called Shoot and Cut. We made a serial that went by the name *Hum Bambai Nahin Jayenge* but unfortunately, the channel shut down; so we directed about 13 or 14 episodes and that was it. Then Shekhar *ji* went away to direct *Elizabeth*. Suddenly, there was nothing to do.

I thought that I would dabble in television. That is when I started with the drama series, *Just Mohabbat*. I did the first eight episodes of this serial but then had a spat with the producer and left it. Then I directed Zee Television's *Naya Daur* based on the Hindi novel by Bhagwati Charan Verma, which lasted for about two years or so. I wrote the dialogues for Mani Ratnam's *Dil Se* (1998). Through Bobby Bedi, I also did casting for films abroad which paid quite well.

Nirmal: *So tell us about your first film* Haasil *(2003).*

Tigmanshu: While I was doing television, I had been writing *Haasil's* script. A great thing that happened to me was the *Star Bestsellers* series on Star TV in 1999. I directed six independent stories/episodes. It provided a platform to showcase something like a short independent film with a beginning, middle and end. Names such as Imtiaz Ali, Anurag Kashyap, Sriram Raghavan and me, we all got a chance to write and direct, thanks to this drama series. We were all involved in television. But back then television was not like it is today. Qualitatively it was better. For one, the serials were weekly and not everyday. Secondly, even that one episode was made like a film. It would be edited repeatedly till it was satisfactory. These days who has the time? The script for the soap opera arrives in the morning and the episode is shot in one day.

I went with the script of *Haasil* to almost every producer in town. Usually, the standard response was that people would ask me to write a script for them and that during that process my film would also get produced. But I did not want it that way. At that point, I reconnected with Bobby Bedi who asked me to direct *Rajdhani* (1999–2000), a serial for Star TV. I made it clear to Bobby that I would just direct the first 10 episodes because I did not want to remain in television. Bobby agreed and promised that he would start the pre-production of my film. So I went to Delhi and when shooting began, it was a rigorous, full-day job. Nothing was happening regarding my film.

I had already decided the climax of my film—at the Kumbh Mela in Allahabad. The *mela* was to take place by the end of the year. I had completed the casting for the movie and finalized Irrfan Khan, Jimmy Shergill, Hrishita Bhatt, Ashutosh Rana and others. Bobby kept postponing my film. I got very agitated and even fought with him over the phone.

A friend of mine, Amrita Sehgal, really supported me during this phase and helped me out financially. The Kumbh Mela was fast approaching, and so with our personal money, we travelled with the actors and completed the big shots with the running crowds and then edited them. It was Mr Vijay Jindal, CEO of Zee Television, who liked the film, sanctioned it and eventually that is how it was made.

Preeti: *If one traces your filmmaking trajectory, starting from* Haasil, *which I see as aspiring to be a commercial success, to* Paan Singh Tomar, *which is such an honest portrayal and does not care about being a hit. The evolution, if I may call it that, is phenomenal. Was this transition a conscious one?*

Tigmanshu: I would love to make a commercial film like *Haasil* even today. My first film was a conscious effort to make a commercial film with songs and *qawwali*, conflict and action. Everybody told me that do not put a *qawwali* in the last scene, but I wanted it done just that way. When I see a film and a *qawwali* comes on the screen, I am reminded of the mingling smells of *samosa* and urine in the theatre. That is the kind of cinema that I want to make.

Source: Authors.

Paan Singh Tomar is a *masala* film. It is about the underdog and therefore connects deeply with an audience. He was tortured and so he picked up a gun, and became a dacoit. That is why it is a success. I am not an Onir. Let me tell you, he is a dear friend. Neither do I see that kind of cinema nor can I make it. I am a Vijay Anand and Raj Khosla fan. I am not a Shyam Benegal fan. I mean there are wonderful films of Benegal, like *Kalyug* and *Jurm*.

Preeti: *But why are there no songs in* Paan Singh Tomar?

Tigmanshu: There are songs in the background. After all, Paan Singh could not be shown singing those songs. That would have been weird. *Paan Singh Tomar* has entertained people. It is not a pretentious film.

Nirmal: *Was there a doubt that a film like* Paan Singh Tomar *might not be a success with the masses?*

Tigmanshu: Yes. UTV put that doubt in me.

Nirmal: Paan Singh Tomar *is similar to a film like* Bandit Queen.

Tigmanshu: If the film *Bandit Queen* had not existed, then *Paan Singh Tomar* would never have been made. While doing research for *Bandit Queen,* I came across an article on Paan Singh and I thought that would make a film on this individual. Also, I would have never been exposed to the terrain, etc., had I not been involved with *Bandit Queen*. The location for shooting was the same.

Preeti: *If you were to make* Haasil *again, what would you do differently?*

Tigmanshu: I would make it more hard core and more violent.

Nirmal: *What is your take on sequels and remakes?*

Tigmanshu: I am fine with both. If you have established a franchise and you want to ride on it then ride on it. As for remakes, I tried making *Sahib, Biwi Aur Gangster*, which is a remake of *Sahib, Biwi Aur Ghulam*. I made it with much trepidation.

Nirmal: *A film like* Paan Singh Tomar *might be more appreciated by an audience that can understand its nuances. But* Sahib, Biwi Aur Gangster *is a masterpiece that touches a raw nerve time and again.*

Tigmanshu: Actually, *Paan Singh Tomar*, box-office wise, performed much more brilliantly than *Sahib, Biwi Aur Gangster*.

Nirmal: What I mean is that with Sahib, Biwi Aur Gangster, *you achieved both commercial and artistic brilliance.*

Tigmanshu: That has always been my goal. I come from the Shekhar Kapur and Mani Ratnam schools of filmmaking. I have worked with both these directors. I want to portray something substantial through my films but make it entertaining too, so that the viewer enjoys himself.

An adaptation, if reproduced as the original, becomes very boring. According to me, the best adaptation of *Devdas* is *Muqaddar ka Sikandar*. I feel that Prakash Mehra was a great filmmaker.

Nirmal: There is a controlled yet absolute sensuality that the character of Mahie Gill exudes throughout the film. There is no skin show, but she is amazingly sensuous. How did you achieve that?

Tigmanshu: Actually, I wanted to remake the 1967 film *Raat Aur Din* (Night And Day). It has Nargis *ji*, Pradeep Kumar and a young Feroz Khan *ji*. The film is about a schizophrenic housewife who is a club-going, cigarette-smoking woman about town by night and a typical middle-class housewife by day. Her husband goes berserk wondering what is happening. I thought this was a modern subject and really wanted to remake this film. The character of Mahie Gill has shades of Nargis's character in *Raat Aur Din*.

For the first time, economics motivated us to make the film that we eventually made. It was made in a budget of 10 million. I did not pay any of the cast or crew before the film was released nor did I take anything myself. I had made it clear to everyone that they would be paid once the film was released and the money started flowing in.

So then the first hurdle was to learn to make a film with a limited budget. I thought that the best thing would be to adopt Mukesh Bhatt's model and come up with a great title for the film. That was when we came up with *Sahib, Biwi Aur Gangster*!

Also, since this was a modern tale, I did not want the character of *Begum* to be passive or muted. I wanted her to portray an aggressive and sexually demonstrative woman.

At the time of conception, we had no script. Before the script, we went to see the location. We had checked out many locations before we found the final one. Producer Rahul Mitra's brother was the Chief Secretary of Tourism, Gujarat, and he suggested we go see the village of Baria. That is where we found this *haveli* and I knew that I would make the film at this location. But the town itself was almost deserted. There were no hotels nearby. I knew that logistically it would be a nightmare to shoot the film here, but my mind was set.

The town was a boring place, and that seething boredom is what you see in the film and what gives the film its flavour.

Preeti: *Your repertoire of films is such that* Sahib, Biwi Aur Gangster *is the only film that portrays a fully fleshed out female character. Otherwise, the choice of subjects is such that men dominate your filmograpy.*

Tigmanshu: In my movies, the subjects are very macho. But in all my films, even if the women characters have less screen time, they are not merely decorative appendages hanging from the hero's arm or meant to be weak. In *Haasil*, Hrishita's character is a strong one. Even in *Charas*, both the female characters are strong women who guide the main plot. In none of my films the female actors are frivolous.

Preeti: *What genre of filmmaking attracts you? I do not see you making a Yash Chopra kind of a movie. Also, do only male-centric subjects attract you?*

Tigmanshu: To start with, what I look at is the atmosphere. If the atmosphere inspires me then I will do it.

Nirmal: *Are you saying that one day you would not mind making a* Dilwale Dulhania Le Jayenge?

Tigmanshu: First of all, you cannot put *Dilwale Dulhania Le Jayenge* and other romantic comedies in the same category. All of Yash Chopra *ji*'s own films are very good, but the films produced by the Yash Raj camp (except maybe *Ishaqzaade*) cannot be compared to *Dilwale Dulhania Le Jayenge*.

I am in the process of making a romantic film called *Milan Talkies* with Imran Khan and Sonakshi Sinha. It is a love story set in a small town. It revolves around the fun, the trials and the fears that beset a couple living in a small town who share small-town values.

Nirmal: *After making films like* Sahib, Biwi Aur Gangster *and* Paan Singh Tomar, *you are now a top director in Bollywood. How do you deal with the high expectations that people have set for you?*

Tigmanshu: Actually, there were high expectations right after *Haasil*, at least in Mumbai. Then after *Charas* was released, I was denounced and abused by all.

Preeti: *At the time when you directed* Haasil, *the film industry was not really conducive to making such films.* Haasil *was a* *one-off film. Now, there are a slew of films that are exciting and dealing with different subjects.*

Tigmanshu: At the risk of sounding pompous, I will say that if there had not been a *Haasil* then there would not be a *Maqbool*. *Haasil* was no doubt a commercial film, but in its treatment it was different. The hero seemed like the villain, while the villain had a tragic flaw.

What I mean is that it was not because of *Haasil* per se that things changed, but that time was such that change was imminent. Even Hrithik Roshan's films (this was an actor who came onto the scene with a bang and destabilized the position of top heroes) were mere flops. During that period, the audience rejected the typical *masala* film. In comparison to those films, *Haasil* was different or at least perceived as such.

Preeti: *But even in* Haasil *there was a certain degree of romanticism.*

Tigmanshu: Yes. But romanticism should be there in a film. What is wrong with romanticism? Why does not NSD admit and absorb good-looking actors? Cinema has to give pleasure.

Nirmal: *I agree with you. Be it good looks or money – both are an anathema to people at NSD.*

Preeti: *Do you think that there is any clear demarcation between the so-called new wave of cinema and commercial cinema in Bollywood? Is it a personal demarcation? For this book, we clearly demarcated directors who are experimenting and making independent cinema and those who we see as out and out commercial. Do you feel that every director aspires to cross the 1,000-million bracket?*

Tigmanshu: The Story is the king. Neither am I currently interested nor will I ever be in the 1,000-million bracket. I will only make films that I want to make. In my earlier films, I had Jimmy Shergill and Irrfan Khan, but if today Saif Ali Khan wants to be part of my film, I will gladly rope him in. That way, my film and what I want to say will reach a larger audience. If because of a star the cost of production increases then so be it. But I do not strive to make a 1,000-million film.

Preeti: *Sure, but stars like these do change the dynamics of 'meaningful cinema'. There will have to be dancing around the trees.*

Tigmanshu: Let me explain—do you have a problem with *Mother India*? No? The film has a number of songs. But there is no film more realistic than *Mother India*. Even Shyam Benegal cannot make a film like *Mother India*. The biggest blockbusters in Bollywood, be it *Pakeezah, Ganga Jamuna, Sholay, Lagaan* or *Gadar*, these are all rooted in a rural ethos and they have songs, but are as realistic as cinema gets. These are good films.

Why do so-called intellectuals and critics deride songs in Bollywood? They should understand that this is Indian cinema. This is what differentiates us from the cinema of other cultures. Something that has to be portrayed in four scenes, we express it through one song. Yes, I agree, songs that are just inserted and do not move the plot forward are useless. A song like, *Pal, pal dil ke paas tum rehti ho* from the movie *Black Mail* moves the story forward with such ease. Director Vijay Anand's film songs are never without a purpose. The song *Tu jahaan jahaan chalega* from *Mera Saaya* beautifully expresses the grief of a husband who has lost his wife.

Preeti: But there are many movies where the music does not contribute to the story's movement in any significant way.

Tigmanshu: But then that is the fault of the filmmaker. The songs are not to be blamed.

Preeti: Do you feel there is a dearth of good storytellers in Bollywood?

Tigmanshu: Yes, these days there is a dearth of good storytelling in Hindi cinema.

Preeti: Why don't directors work with adaptations? At least the story will be sound. Be it adaptations of former films or from literature.

Tigmanshu: The films that are being churned out today are products of cinema, and not products of life. That is the real problem. These films are not rooted. In comparison to Hindi cinema, films emerging from Southern India are far more rooted, far more entertaining and they have a loyal fan following. South Indian directors are better storytellers.

I, myself, am adapting Amritlal Nagar's novel, *Saat Ghunghat Wala Mukhada*, which is based on the life of Begum Samru. I need time to make a heroine-oriented, period film because such a film needs a big budget. But I will definitely make the film.

There is also the issue of 'what was your last hit' in our film industry. There is a norm in Bollywood that period films do not sell. *Mangal Pandey: The Rising* was a bad picture. *Jodhaa Akbar* received a lukewarm reception. Ultimately, everything depends on numbers.

Nirmal: How do you choose your production team? Do you take decisions regarding the type of camera, the type of lens, filter and lighting that will be used during shooting?

Tigmanshu: I always prefer to work with my friends. Whenever I have worked with others, I have faced problems. For example, during the shooting of *Paan Singh Tomar*, initially, I started working with a cameraman, who I thought was highly competent in visuals. He turned out to be lax; he would take a shot and then talk on the phone. So that is when I approached Aseem Mishra.

Yes, I am specific about everything. For example, *Sahib, Biwi Aur Gangster* was shot on the Elixir digital camera that was used for the first time in India. I used it because it would bring down the production cost.

Preeti: *What, according to you, is the basic skill set required for becoming a director? We have an industry that has formally trained filmmakers as well as those who learn on the set.*

Tigmanshu: *Ishq*. What you need to know is love in order to learn anything. When Bobby Bedi gave me the six-part episode, *Krishna's Dream*, to direct for Channel Four, when shooting began I was quite green even though I had ADs. This was at Delhi's Marwah Studios with a train set laid out. While shooting, you have to complete all the shots for one location in one stretch so that lighting, etc., does not have to be set up again. I did not know this. The cameraperson, who belonged to Delhi and was a reputed pass out from FTII, took me to a corner and told me that if I was going to function in this manner, he would not work with me. The next day I was on the set at six in the morning. I worked out the plan for the day's shooting on a piece of paper, and everything was fine after that.

So I knew what had to be done, but faced problem in execution. I made a mistake but quickly learned from it.

Nirmal: *Will cinema with a limited viewership, the sort screened only in the multiplexes (be it Dibakar Banerjee's films or Onir's* *films) survive the onslaught of big 'blockbuster' films such as* Dabangg *or* Singham? *For that matter even your films have mass appeal and perform well at the box office.*

Tigmanshu: Both these kinds of cinemas have always coexisted and will continue to do so.

Nirmal: But they will not get space in the multiplex. A big film will take four screens.

Tigmanshu: Yes, that is true. What happened in the case of *Paan Singh Tomar* was that UTV had already sold the satellite rights for the film. So they did a low-key release for the film with just 250 screens. These were all digital prints. There was not even one physical print. Eventually, they increased the number of screens by 100 or so because of strong word-of-mouth advertising. In the case of *Sahib, Biwi Aur Gangster,* since I was its producer, it was released in 700 screens.

About the Authors

Nirmal Kumar is Associate Professor of History at Sri Venkateswara College, University of Delhi. He has been working on 18th-century Rajasthan and also on Hindi films. He has co-edited a book *Filming the Line of Control* for Routledge in 2008. Two of his books are under publication: *Essays in History of Early Modern India* and *Medieval Delhi: A Reader*. He is also the General Editor of a series on *Historians of Medieval India*.

Dr Kumar is widely travelled and well networked with renowned institutions worldwide. He is fellow of the Royal Asiatic Society of Great Britain and Ireland and Member of the Women's History Network, UK. He is also associated with the Society for South Asian Studies, London, and British Association of South Asian Studies, UK. He is on the Board of Contemporary India Study Center Aarhus, Aarhus University, Denmark, and a guest fellow at the Indian Institute of Advanced Study, Shimla (2012). Besides, he takes keen interest in Bihar, his home state in India, and is an ace photographer.

Preeti Chaturvedi is a senior marketing professional and writes on media and cultural studies. She has co-authored India's first book on blogging, *Corporate Blogging in India* (2009). Preeti's blog 'Checkposts' features amongst the leading marketing blogs in the country. Preeti has contributed to global research on branding and has published papers with Brandchannel.com and World Advertising Research Center. She has also written extensively on media, marketing and cultural studies for the ICFAI Press, Indian Council for Cultural Relations, Moneycontrol.com, *Business and Economy*.

A Delhi University topper in English Literature from Miranda House with an Executive Diploma in Sales and Marketing from the Indian Institute of Management (IIM), Calcutta, she has also been a guest faculty/speaker at leading institutes like the IIT and Fore School of Management. She has a decade of experience in marketing communications during which she has handled some of the leading global brands.